Dollars to Dignity

UNRAVELLING THE MONEY AND SELF ESTEEM PARADOX

بِسْمِ ٱللّٰهِ ٱلرَّحْمٰنِ ٱلرَّحِيمِ

Dollars to Dignity

UNRAVELLING THE MONEY AND SELF ESTEEM PARADOX

Authored By,

BADAR ARSHI

Disclaimer

This book has been published with all reasonable efforts taken to make the material error-free after the consent of the author. This book is sold subject to the condition that it shall not, by way of trade or otherwise, be lent, resold, or otherwise circulated without the copyright owner's prior written consent in any form of binding or cover other than that in which it is published and without a similar condition including this condition being imposed on the subsequent purchaser and without limiting the rights under copyright reserved above, no part of this publication maybe reproduced, stored in or introduced into a retrieval system or transmitted in any form or by any other means without the permission of the copyright owner.

Registered Office- 907-Sneh Nagar, Sapna Sangeeta Road,
Agrasen Square, Indore – 452001 (M.P.), India

Website: http://www.wingspublication.com

Email: mybook@wingspublication.com

First Published by WINGS PUBLICATION 2024

Copyright © BADAR ARSHI

Title : Dollars to Dignity

Price : AED 60.00 I $ 20.00 I PKR 2,300

All Rights Reserved.

ISBN : 978-93-6006-468-6

LIMITS OF LIABILITY/DISCLAIMER OF WARRANTY

The Author of this book is solely responsible and liable for its content including but not limited to the views, representations, descriptions, statements, information, opinions and references. The information presented in this book is solely compiled by the Author from sources believed to be accurate and the Publisher assumes no responsibility for any errors or omissions. The information is not intended to replace or substitute professional advice.

The Content of this book shall not constitute or be construed or deemed to reflect the opinion or expression of the Publisher. Publisher of this book does not endorse or approve any content of this book or guarantee the reliability, accuracy or completeness of the content published herein and do not make any representations or warranties of any kind, express or implied, including but not limited to the implied warranties of merchantability, fitness for a particular purpose. The Publisher shall not be held liable whatsoever for any errors, omissions, whether such errors or omissions result from negligence, accident, or any other cause or claims for loss or damages of any kind, including without limitation, indirect or consequential loss or damage arising out of use, inability to use, or about the reliability, accuracy or sufficiency of the information contained in this book. All disputes are subject to Indore (M.P.) jurisdiction only.

DEDICATION

This book is dedicated to the human race
who have kept the ray of hope lit in their eyes
for a respectable and prosperous life despite the
worst economic circumstances, that has made
it absolutely impossible to keep the relation
of body and soul intact.

Disclaimer

This book is not a magic wand or a guarantee of success. I don't know you and your potential and the intensity of your desire to succeed, so I can't promise your success. However, I do know that if you work hard, sincerely and passionately, you will get a better start than most. What I can do is to provide you a road map. In the end, it's up to you to take action. Your success is determined by YOUR desire, teachability and willingness to work.

The facts, figures, opinions and information presented in this book and the views of the author are as of the date of publication, which is gathered through extensive research. The various sources used among others are international magazines, books, newspapers, world wide web, opinions of renowned economists and experienced industry masters.

Because of the rate with which conditions change, the author reserves the right to alter and update his opinion based on the new conditions.

The book is for informational purposes only. Copyright permission is granted neither in whole nor in part unless it is expressly granted by the author.

BEGINNING OF THE JOURNEY

A journey of thousand miles begins with the first step
(Lao-Tzu)

First step begins with a thought
(Badar Arshi)

REVIEWS AND TRIBUTES FOR "DOLLARS TO DIGNITY"

'Dollars to Dignity' is a groundbreaking exploration of wealth's true essence. Through vivid storytelling and profound insights, it illuminates the intrinsic connection between financial empowerment and human dignity. This transformative narrative transcends conventional wisdom, urging readers to reevaluate their perceptions of success and worth. With empathy as its guiding light, the book inspires introspection and societal change, offering a roadmap towards a more equitable world. A must-read for anyone seeking to understand the profound impact of money on our lives and the power of reclaiming dignity in every aspect of our existence.

Andy Harington
Founder of Professional Speakers Academy

This is a must have book for everyone in today's era. It is so important to be able to live with the pace that the world is changing at most of us are lacking behind others. The competition is more than ever and this book will help you win, not only at this competition of life, but in every aspect.

Dr. Deepak Parbat
Best Selling Author of "Well Done You Are Hired" and "A Monk In Suit"

'Dollars to Dignity' is a game-changer! This book offers a refreshing perspective on financial empowerment, blending practical advice with a focus on self-worth and personal growth. It's a must-read for anyone looking to transform their relationship with money and achieve true financial independence. Highly recommended for its actionable insights and inspiring approach to wealth creation.

Mian Nabeel Ashraf
Managing Director & CEO Air Falcon

In the age where everyone is struggling to do the same things, how does one stand out? If you have the guidance of this book, then you will be the one that stands out. This book will help you achieve extraordinary success and change your life for the better.

Ms. Manika Singh
Best Selling Author of "Decoding Fitness" and "Chakra Entrepreneur"

'Dollars to Dignity' is a powerful and inspiring guide to financial empowerment. The author's holistic approach to wealth creation, which emphasizes self-worth and personal growth, is both practical and illuminating. 'Dollars to Dignity' is a beacon of insight and empowerment in today's materialistic world. With gripping narratives and profound wisdom, it unveils the intrinsic link between wealth and human dignity. It challenges societal norms, ignites introspection, and guides readers towards a more fulfilling life beyond monetary measures. A captivating journey that redefines success, urging us to embrace empathy and equality.

I highly recommend 'Dollars to Dignity' to anyone seeking a fresh and empowering perspective on their financial journey.

Nadeem Zia
Founder and CEO of R&N Global Solutions.

This book should be considered revolutionary. This book has the power to change the life entirely for anyone who commits to it. Once the reader commits to the tips and techniques given in this book, there is nothing that will stop them from being their best version and succeed at any endeavour that they undertake.

Shivangi Desai
Health and Nutrition Coach
Best Selling Author of "Beyond Verses" and "Holistic Health"

MONEY AND SELF-ESTEEM

In a world often driven by material wealth and superficial success, this book offers a refreshing perspective on what it truly means to live a dignified life.

Through eloquent prose and poignant storytelling, the author navigates the complexities of human existence, illuminating the profound connection between financial empowerment and personal dignity. 'Dollars to Dignity' is a manifesto for reclaiming our sense of worth and purpose in a society that too often measures value in monetary terms alone.

What sets this book apart is its unwavering commitment to compassion and empathy. With each page, I found myself nodding in agreement and ultimately, emerging with a renewed sense of clarity and purpose.

Whether you're grappling with financial hardship, seeking meaning beyond material possessions, or simply yearning for a more equitable world, 'Dollars to Dignity' is a must-read.

I wholeheartedly recommend it to anyone ready

to embark on a journey of self-discovery and empowerment."

Ather H. Medina
CEO Habib Metropolitan Financial Services

Acknowledgements

This book took a lot of pain, research and hundreds of non-slept hours. It was the labour of love and took the combined efforts of many people. I especially wish to acknowledge the following.

- To my father from heavenly abode, whose presence I feel is always with me. Who is the main source and inspiration for me to face and overcome life challenges! His life struggles, encouraged me to help others.

- To my mother, who always pray for my success and extend her warm affections to me, which gives me the drive to do better things for people.

- To my wife and my children for supporting me in my writing journey despite difficult circumstances and giving valuable input and ideas. I am obliged to them.

- To Dr. Kailash Pinjani for continuously injecting energy boosters and ideas and providing immaculate and unwavering support and encouragement.

- To all the people who have provided valuable feedback, comments, and testimonials,

Thanks, and love to all.

Foreword

It is a hard era to be living in. Our lives are upturned everyday with new technological developments and it's creating a feeling of unsettlement among people. The world seems to change overnight and it is difficult to be able to keep up with everything that is happening in the world.

What to do in a situation where you have no security about your future? This book is the answer. This book decodes and breaks down all the possible and secure future options, life changing lessons and a vulnerable account of Mr. Badar that I'm sure is relatable to anyone reading this book.

Reading this book is a life changing experience, and not only in terms of a phrase. This book will actually help the reader change the dynamic of their life and be able to move forward and ahead of their stagnant insecure lifestyle. This book will motivate you to take action, change your current state and live your best life.

Living in the fear of the future will ruin your present prospects at life. Take this book to the T and you will notice a sizable change in your life and the life of everyone around you. I only hope that this book reaches everyone who is looking to improve their life and will be able to reap the benefit of the hard work that Mr. Badar has put into the making of this book.

Dr. Kailash Pinjani
Best Selling Author of **"Date Your Clients"** and **"Catch The Shark"**

About the Author

Badar Arshi is a Chartered Accountant by profession. He has also earned the qualifications of Cost and Management Accountancy and Master of Business Administration. He served as corporate executive in the Middle Eastern Gulf Aviation Industry for over 20 years.

He had extensively traveled around the world and gained extensive learning experience, studying and researching business trends and models. He is a Certified Master Life Coach, Motivational Speaker and a Certified Business Trainer, a self-esteem facilitator and conduct trainings at national and international levels. He is great enthusiast and loud voice supporting human development, growth and self-esteem. His main life project & area of interest is human consciousness. He helps people understand that they are here in this world, not by an accident or by a chance. But they are a direct result of a deliberate and conscious decision, to be choice making & free will human beings, unlike other programmed creatures, and therefore their self-esteem is the most valuable asset that they have, not to be compromised ever.

He has an inborn sense of idealism and morality without being an idle dreamer, capable of taking concrete steps to realize the goals and make a lasting positive impact. **He is attracted to the idea of egalitarianism and believe that nothing would help the world as much as love and compassion.**

His purpose and mission of life is to help people achieve financial freedom and break the debt trap;

He can be reached at badararshi@gmail.com

About the Book

The main message of "Dollars to Dignity" revolves around the intricate relationship between financial status, materialism, and self-worth. The book delves into how money influences self-esteem, decision-making processes, and social interactions, highlighting the psychological aspects of how individuals perceive themselves in relation to their financial status.

The target audience for the book "Dollars to Dignity" likely includes individuals interested in understanding the complex interplay between financial status, materialism, and self-worth. It may also appeal to individuals looking to explore the relationship between financial wealth and self-perception. Additionally, those who are interested in self-improvement and social psychology could find the book insightful and thought-provoking.

The book "Dollars to Dignity" offers readers several benefits, including deeper understanding of how money influences self-esteem, decision making processes, and social interactions. The book likely empowers readers to improve their self-esteem by taking actionable steps and serve as a guide for readers on attracting wealth by enhancing their self-esteem.

Contents

PART 1 - PSYCHOANALYSIS OF LIFE MISERIES

Introduction

Most books are written just to satisfy peoples reading pleasure. This one is written to be used! and change the life of the READER.

"Dollars" denote MONEY and "Dignity" denotes, human SELF-ESTEEM. How the human life is entangled between this loop is the main crux of this book.

This book is based on my first-hand experience of the circumstances described throughout the pages, which I have gone through in life journey. I can certainly relate it to the situation of most of the people out there. Certain thoughts and ideas were just revealed as diamond cognitions from the heavenly realm. I am sure you will find valuable advice, food for thought, and logical career explanations in this book, which you can look at before placing it on your bookshelf. In order to get the best results, YOU MUST use them repeatedly throughout your life. Here is how you should do this:

- Find a peaceful, comfortable and private place so that you should not be disturbed while reading.

- Keep a paper and pencil with you.

- Read the entire book. (Not necessarily in one sitting)

- Visualize the situations discussed during the reading and link them with yours if they relate.

- Make important points.

- Make an honest and concrete decision to change the present situation of your life.

- Pass on this book to someone you love and care about, so that it can change his or her LIFE as well.

The world economy has seen many ups and downs through the decades. The business and trade practices, which started on barter basis centuries ago, are now experiencing e-commerce and the Internet revolution. Never before has the world been struck with the worst economic situation, this era is passing through. The level of unemployment, job insecurities, pay cutoffs, downsizing, layoffs, golden shake hands, etc., are the terms people were unaware of a decade ago. They have started looking for alternatives for survival. Home-based businesses, second incomes, and backup financial arrangements are the main concerns of today. Due to the poor purchasing power of people, conventional businesses are finding it difficult to sell their products by spending heavily on advertisements & traditional distribution methods, which add up the product costs substantially.

The introduction of technology-based production techniques on one hand resulted in quantum increase in production, and on the other hand have made hundreds and thousands of people redundant, and pushed them to the wall in the war of survival.

In the following pages, we will discuss, among others:

- The human design
- Purpose and meaning of life

- Mysteries of belief and thought

- The luck design

- Wealth creation framework

We hope that this book will help hundreds and thousands of people who still have hope in their eyes to become successful in life and will bring smiles to their faces.

> **"Humans get bored of childhood, they hurry to grow up, then they long to be children again. They think about the future with anxiety and forget the present. They neither live in the present nor the future. They live as they will never die. They die as if they had never lived."**
>
> **(Khalil Jibran)**

PART 1

PSYCHOANALYSIS OF LIFE MISERIES

Chapter 1

Money and Self-Esteem

Idea "Human" is the biggest project of the universe. To date, humankind remains a mystery to itself. Majestic divinity and Human dignity are aligned to fill this world with abundance, happiness and prosperity. Let human esteem arise, let it arise to meet the heights of the highest sublime Majestic-Esteem.

The human soul has three components, Energy, Esteem and Eternity. Esteem is the central part of human design. All the creations are subordinate to human greatness and every human child who appears in this world is housed with esteem as a fundamental human right. The fact that human esteem is important cannot be denied or escaped.

Self-esteem is a key human need irrespective of our ignorance or awareness of its operational dynamics, it is an insight realization and trust in self-ability that we are competent and deserve to be equipped and decorated with the unique attributes of "consciousness and choice".

Self-esteem is highly sensitive to different situations and circumstances and reacts to multiple factors, like:

Self-Esteem Influencing Factors	
■ Money	■ Family background & status
■ Brought up environment	■ Education
■ Capability & competence	■ Position
■ Appearance	■ Culture & Society
■ Social comparison	■ Purpose

Among all, MONEY is the most powerful factor, which in many circumstances is directly linked with the level of human self-esteem and has the power to influence and impact other self-esteem factors as well.

Money the Currency of Life

In the economic terms, money denotes a value which is used as a medium to exchange goods and services. The social concept of money symbolizes power, authority, status, respect, security, command and control.

Money once a facilitator to replace the exchange of goods under barter system becomes a symbol of power status and respect. The talented, noble, honest and educated who have limited money are looked down upon. The standards of human dignity and nobility are changed and measured through the weight of gold, diamonds and the amount of money one has.

Money is undeniably necessary for all of us. We need money to have roof on our head, food on the table for survival, and clothing to cover. Without meeting the basics needs, the life would be in serious trouble. Money is the resource that allows us to attain a certain level of security and safety.

In the absence of sufficient money, our living options are restricted to where we can live, what we can eat, and how we can spend our time. It takes the soul out when we're worried about how we'll make our car instalment this month.

Is Money Really Important?

Whenever the topic of money is discussed, these questions are always surfaced,

IS MONEY IMPORTANT?

IS MONEY REALLY GOOD?

IS MONEY NECESSARY?

IS POVERTY VIRTUOUS?

Ask a person who has not eaten in two days.

I would like to begin with a passage from the book "THINK AND GROW RICH" By Napoleon Hill. In which the case of money is presented as below:

"Does success only refer to accumulating cash? Millions of individuals will say, "Give me all the money I need and I will find everything else I want," despite the fact that there are undoubtedly many things that are more valuable than money.

The fear of poverty, which has the power to paralyze millions of men and women, can affect anyone at any time. Money cannot purchase many riches from the heart and soul, yet most people are too poor to remember this and feel uplifted. A man's slumped shoulders, and the worn hat, the way he walks, and the way he looks all reveal something about the state of his spirit while he is jobless and living on the streets. Even while he knows that those who have normal jobs are not in any way comparable to him in terms of intelligence, character, or talent, he is unable to shake the sensation that he is inferior to them.

However, these people, even his friends, feel superior to him and, maybe unintentionally, see him as a victim. He is allowed to borrow money temporarily but not indefinitely. The act of borrowing just to make ends meet might be a disheartening one. The ability to restore one's spirits is not possessed by borrowed money. For individuals with high bravery, noble values, and self-respect, it is not the cure for the ongoing scars and failures.

A man who is jobless and depressed has nothing to do. He walks great distances in the hope of finding employment, but his efforts are in vain, or he ends up working in a position where the only pay is a commission on the sale of worthless things that nobody wants to buy except for a small group of pious buyers.

He returns to the streets, having nowhere to go, but continues to stroll. He feels inadequate as he looks inside the windows of elegantly designed stores at the luxuries that are out of his price range and makes way for others who are actively interested in making purchases. He strolls along train tracks or visits a library to take a little break from the grind, but he isn't getting work, so he moves on. He is blind to the fact that his meaningless existence is robbing him of his dreams. Even if he dresses well, from his days of stable employment, his falling shoulders will still be visible.

He is envious of thousands of other people, including book salesmen, clerks, chemists, and car owners, and feels nothing but envy for them. They are healthy, independent, and respected, but he just can't make himself believe that he's a good man too. This difference in him was only brought about by money, and with a little more, he could return to his regular life and become himself once more".

They say money can buy golden beds but not sleep, buy food but not appetite, buy medicines but not health! My question is if your son or mother is on the death bed, dying just because you cannot afford their treatment, and just a few thousand bucks can save them from a premature death in front of your eyes. Knowing that, would you be able to sleep? Would you feel hungry and wanted to eat? Would your health remain normal? Will you still believe that poverty is better than being filthy rich? How do you feel if your father or husband is insulted by the bank's recovery officer or the lender or the landlord for just not being able to pay the loan instalment or the monthly rent? How will you feel if the school or college cancels the admission of your sweet daughter or hero son just because you are not able to pay the semester fees? And how do you feel if your kid or wife stops talking to you with respect or your in-laws make you feel down because you are unable to buy their daughter a decent house with that extra separate room or that gadget on their birthday or how do you feel if your best friend or sister request you to lend them some amount and you have to refuse them. Do you still feel that being poor is noble and poverty is glory?

Sure, there are lot of other factors which affect your "self-esteem" but money is more lethal. It does something to your soul which takes out the feeling within you, that you are also a good person and deserves respect. There is a strong link between money and self-esteem.

They say rich people seize and take away our resources, exploit the underprivileged people and use them for their evil designs. They are corrupt, but there are rich people who fund charities and donate huge amounts to build hospitals and institutions and establish corporations and provide millions of jobs. Are filthy rich people really filthy and bad? They say Money is the root of all evil, is money really that bad? Money is neither bad nor good; money is neutral in its essence. It is just like any other tool or medium. If it is in the hands of good people, it is good and if it is in the hands of bad people, it is bad. Money is not the root of all evil, but poverty is.

Poverty is inhumane. Poverty is bad and debt is worst, a new form of human slavery. A few moments of bad decision can last an entire life long anguish. Poverty exerts a painful influence over our lives.

Many aspects of our lives are impacted by money. One could argue that some of our most memorable events were made possible by the money we had to spend on them. On the other side, our financial circumstances might cause us a great deal of tension and worry.

Without adequate money, our freedoms are restricted, and we even have to work long hours to make ends meet. This is why having money is crucial since it provides us with control and freedom. We feel helpless in the face of our limited control on life.

The reason money extremely matters in life is that it provides us with options; the more money we have, the more options we have. The sense of security that comes with having money allows us to make wise financial decisions since it assures us that a minor issue won't snowball into a major one.

Our health is impacted by money. Anxiety and sadness are frequently brought on by financial stress. Some people become a victim mindset in resentment. Many decide to give up on their dreams of ever paying off their debt or landing a better career. Prolonged stress can cause physical health issues like weight gain, sleeplessness, heart attack risk, and immune system weakness.

Money is significant since it is a quick and easy solution to a lot of life's issues.

If you've never been content with your financial situation, you may view money as a rare resource. Alternatively, you may look at it as something unattainable.

Money has a big impact on how each of us lives. It has the power to present incredible opportunities that can completely alter our life's trajectory.

Therefore, it's critical to have the correct mindset toward money and recognize the genuine worth of money in life and the opportunities it can present when you have a positive image on its significance. You'll come to understand that money is really an impartial, limitless resource to help you and not to bring you misery.

The most important opinion.

Have you ever heard people saying statements like, I do not have sufficient means, I do not have capabilities & skills, I am unlucky, I have never got any opportunity and chance in life, I do not know anyone influential or some big shot, I do not have favourable circumstances and fair environment, no matter how much hard work I do, I don't get results, Divine has chosen and destined me to fail and suffer etc.?

Write it on concrete, or with gold. The most important opinion in your life, is the opinion you have about your own self. The opinion which can move the mountains, the opinion that you are significant and valuable. The opinion that you are competent to encounter the challenges life throws at you.

Every human child born and every human soul created has an inherent birthright to be respected. When we landed on this Earth, we were all the same. Our environment, our beliefs and our experiences, which were given to us, made all the difference.

"It's not what you are that holds you back, it's what you think you're not."

Denis Waitley

A high sense of self-worth is the basis for all of your chosen thoughts, beliefs, emotions, and actions about yourself, how you interact with others, and what you think about as you attract, create, and experience the different events, conditions, and situations you go through in life.

The choices we make about our self-esteem, affects and decide the quality of every part of our lives, including our health, finances, relationships and feelings.

From the time we are very young, we are taught in many different ways to "believe" that we are not worthwhile, not good enough, or flawed in some way or other. We learn and hold the "belief" that getting what we want is "hard" and not possible. This kind of conditioning can and often does happen in the nicest ways and with the best of intentions, but it still happens. And we've let it happen.

We are told and, most of the time, "believe" that we are flawed and limited. What's reasonable, sensible, useful, and "doable or not doable" is "taught" to us. So, we make our lives and experience them in a way that fits with what we've decided. Because we don't know why we believe what we believe, we live our lives "unconsciously creating" and don't see how our personal power, what we "know and believe" to be true, is making the world around us the way we want it to be.

How is it that having a good opinion of yourself is so important for finding balance, happiness, fulfilment, and plenty in life?

Once you know that everything, seen and unseen, is made up of pure energy and that all energy has a certain frequency that determines the quality of life and how these energies bring the events, conditions, and circumstances that happen to you in your daily life, you will know how important it is to have high self-esteem.

We believe that what we think about ourselves and what we think we can or cannot do sets the "projected frequency." The frequency's quality depends on the quality of the beliefs we choose.

Money and self-esteem connection

There is a direct, strong connection between money and self-esteem:

In a society that heavily emphasizes material success, one's ability to earn money and support oneself financially contributes greatly to the feelings of self-worth and confidence. Being highly compensated is equated with the value and competence of a person.

Having enough money to consistently meet one's basic needs without significant worry or stress contributes to a strong sense of self-esteem and self-efficacy. Not having to constantly be in survival financial mode is freedom.

Increased income gives people greater options, freedom, power to make confident decisions, and overall independence in determining the trajectory of their lives. This autonomy boosts self-regard and esteem.

Huge wealth, extravagant goods, positions, titles, and big donations attract more respect and admiration. Many adopt their social status as a part of their identity. These realities deeply connect money with self-esteem.

People work hard to achieve financial success. Money is crucial to meet basic human requirements like feeding and housing. People use number of cognitive biases to maintain a favorable self-image. They typically believe they are above average than others in intelligence, morality, and generosity. Capability and competency are vital components of self-esteem, and the ability to earn money demonstrates their competence. People want monetary rewards along with maintaining a favorable self-image. Money and self-esteem are two important things that people need, desire, and strive for. People are more satisfied when they earn money through their own efforts rather than when they receive unemployment allowances. Losing a job reduces life happiness because it prevents people from earning an income and jeopardizes their sense of self-worth. Unemployment compensation has a negative impact on the receiver's self-concept and self-esteem. Improved financial circumstances boost self-esteem. Social comparison is a valuable reference point. People feel better about themselves when they outperform others. This is possibly because comparative income has a greater influence on self-esteem than absolute income. Affiliation with a valuable group and being acknowledged as an important member of a club or institution also contribute to high self-esteem. Research has shown that those with high-trait self-esteem have more resources available to them to maintain their positive self-esteem than those with low-trait self-esteem.

The Pinnacle of Self-Esteem - Beyond Maslow

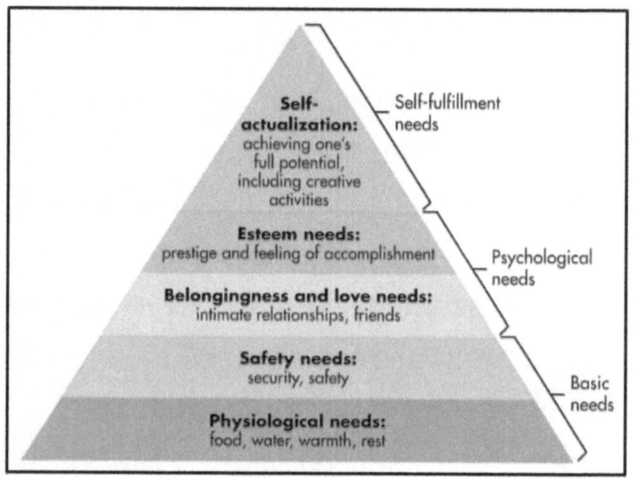

Abraham Maslow, when presented his famous hierarchy of needs, placed self-esteem at the fourth level and food and water at the first level. Once the first-level needs are satisfied, then, people move on to the second level, and so on. This is where Maslow overlooked the mystery of self-esteem operating at the level of high trait. My question is that, with a high trait self-esteem if food is thrown in front of you, will you pick it up and eat? Obviously, you'll reject it as an insult and prefer to remain hungry. This is where

Maslow miscalculated the functioning of human emotions, while explaining the human psychology and overlooked to built them in his model.

Some may argue that yes, some people will pick up the food and prefer to save their life and satisfy their survival need, like we do see that in not too distant past, slaves do pick up the bread thrown in front of them. Do you think they were doing this with having high trait self-esteem? Of course not. They were operating at a level with either deactivated self-esteem or low trait self-esteem. At which level do you think you are operating at?

Again, in history, we have seen that on the battlefield, when a dying wounded soldier is offered water, he signalled to give it to his fellow wounded soldier lying next to him, and when water was presented to the next soldier, he signalled it to pass it on to the next soldier lying on the ground wounded. And when the water reached him, he was already dead, then when water came to the previous soldier, he was dead too, then to the earlier one and the first one, they were all dead. What does this all mean? Self-actualization! over their basic survival needs. How humans can work like this. Till date, humankind remains a mystery to itself and will remain a mystery, not to blame Maslow.

The universe is created with abundant wealth for the service and pleasure of its creations.

Wealth should not be stockpiled and saturated between few pockets. It must flow freely and shared among all the creatures indiscriminately. In order to achieve this, wealth must be created and poverty must be eradicated.

Commercial activity has a distinct capability and competence to create wealth. It has an established supremacy to pull people out of dearth and poverty. Caring is not a choice but an obligation which should be built into every wealth-creation project and endeavour.

> **"Like slavery and apartheid, poverty is not natural. It is man-made, and it can be overcome and eradicated through the actions of human beings."**
>
> **(Nelson Mandela)**

Chapter 2

Sorrowful Echoes

The study of humans over a period of time reveals that humans have forgotten and overlooked that they are the most independent species in the universe with the choice and wisdom to shape their own lives. Ironically humans create sufferings for themselves and then try to shift the cause to Divine Supreme or Universe for their suffering.

The pain of people

The concept of labour slavery travelled into the industrialization culture managed by family cartels. Employees are treated as slaves by control mechanisms.

People fear downsizing, layoffs, and buyouts by potential companies. They know their actual worth is disregarded, but they still fear being evicted. Talented people oversaturate the labour market, making it easier for employers to replace them with workers who are ready to take less money. On the other side, many who have survived reductions are afraid of having to take on more work without getting paid extra. It's depressing to be the last person standing on a sinking ship, and job stability seems unreal. In actuality, businesses treat their workers like commodities, purchasing them wholesale and reselling them at retail for as long as it is profitable to do so.

Some serious questions:

Why you have to plead and beg for a day-off from the "almighty boss." Why you can't take off any day you choose?

You work 50 weeks a year for the company - and you get only two weeks a year for yourself. Does that seem fair?

Does your boss laugh every time you ask for a raise? Why…?

Our parents told us what to do. Our teachers told us what to do. Now our bosses are telling us what to do. When is it our turn to choose what we want to do?

Why do individuals put up with these conditions?

Many feel stuck, in debt, and forced to take up with abuse because they don't know how else to live. An increasing number of people are filing for bankruptcy, which forces them to give up control of their lives to their employers, who decide how valuable they are. Time is managed; arriving late causes problems; staying late to work is expected. Sundays are hated because they mean that the same exhausting routine will soon resume.

People realize they are living like rats after spending a lot of time trying to win a rat race. According to career adviser Tom Welch, more than 80% of people have jobs they detest or even despise. They secretly long for significance and fulfilment but feel that in order for the company to succeed, they must give up their sense of self-worth.

People may lean behind closed doors, yelling silently in annoyance and a sense of being trapped. Although it's customary to express gratitude for one's employment, many are fed up with chasing after illusory claims of pay increases and promotions. Office politics are valued more highly than talents and abilities in this environment, which depletes people's energy.

Because of the severe effects on mental health, many people turn to imagination in TV shows and movies for comfort. This worrying surge in young-age suicides is partly caused by a declining mental state of mind that shows up as low self-worth, low self-confidence, and a negative self-image.

People live under their own dictators despite the appearance of freedom, with employers setting their vacation schedules, retirement plans, and daily schedules. Dreams of a better future disappear, to be replaced with ugly habits and an ongoing financial burden. There is widespread financial uncertainty, with many people dreading homelessness just a few paychecks away and living paycheck to paycheck. A sizeable portion will rely on friends and family in their later years, and some will work past retirement because they haven't saved enough money.

Given that, luck may be their only chance of salvation, it makes sense that so many people resort to the lottery due to the prevailing sense of hopelessness and the need for a route out. Given these conditions, it makes sense if you, like many others, are experiencing depression.

Put an end to your frustrations and improve your life.

There are others who have been in your shoes before, questioning the same things you are and wanting to know the truth. You'll discover exactly how to put a stop to your annoyances and improve your family's quality of life right here.

FREEDOM IS NOT FREE! The only free cheese is in the mousetrap!

Monozygotic

These two brothers were born from a single ovum at the same time; one was extremely wealthy, well-off, and healthy, while the other was impoverished, deprived, and ill. "Why are you in a state that you are in?" a man questioned the disadvantaged brother. And he answered, "I am where I am because my father was poor, and it led me to poverty". The wealthier brother was asked the same question by the same individual; and guess what he said! "My father was poor is the reason I am where I am because I hated that situation to be in".

This is the key to both poverty and success, a topic we will cover in depth. The same conditions, same situation, and identical circumstances but with distinct results. Is it fate, design, natural unfairness, or something else entirely?

Who's Responsible?

If you are reading this book, great chances are that you want to change your circumstances and your life. The daily struggles you undergo, there are numerous questions about your life, your pain, and your aspirations. What challenges do you face and where do you feel most hurt? Desperately seeking something more, what will your life look like in the next five years? Can you attain financial freedom, liberating yourself from perpetual money worries? Will your circumstances improve, or will they continue with the same challenges? Will you have more time to spend with your family, or will family bonds erode under the weight of stress, leading to constant conflicts?

This is the terrible reality that many people have to live with. It's a dark age with no hope.

How many people get up every day feeling passionate, happy, filled with enthusiasm and excited about what lies ahead? Very few. Most people are exhausted in the mornings and fear the day that lies ahead. They force themselves to get out of bed and go to work, where they frequently feel that loyalty is a one-way path. It is incredibly insecure to know that the firm they have dedicated their lives to, can fire them at any time. Despite the organization proclaiming the virtues of devotion, loyalty, and teamwork, the truth is that workers frequently feel disposable and expendable.

Now having said that the big question is, if your circumstances are not favorable, if this is not the life you want, if things are not going your way, WHO is the architect of it, who is responsible for this, who has created this life of yours, who is in-charge of your life. And most importantly can it still be changed?

Let's explore this and find out if there are actual, justifiable reasons behind it. For a long time, I've been studying the distinctions between EXCUSES and the actual causes behind the outcomes of these affairs.

An excuse absolves you from accountability and suggests that you are not responsible for a situation, and there is nothing you can do about it. You are not to be blamed for it. A strong powerful excuse serves to reduce one's accountability. If you are able to make others believe that your excuse is valid and they accept it then you are released from your responsibility.

One of my favourite limitations and constraints is that my life is where it is because I am too occupied and do not have time to change it, or I do not have the financial resources and means to turn it around. Not convincing enough, ok then maybe it is because I am not well, I am ill, my health is not good, that's power full, people can sympathize with you, poor soul he is not keeping well and can't do much about it, the moment your inability is validated by others a great pressure is removed from your chest that you are not responsible for your circumstances.

And the best one is, fate and destiny, DEITY have destined me to be in this situation and designed my life like what it is. No one can argue with that, it is the act of the divine, how can he go against the will of supreme? As soon as you get the "Certificate of FATE Victim" from others, the blame shifts from you to the divine supreme, to nature, to the universe, to the people out there as they are all acting and ganging up against you according to the fate blueprint.

Every justification someone makes reduces their influence and control over the situation gradually. You turn into a victim after you've effectively communicated the boundaries of your limitation, the pressure is not anymore to change.

It's painful and brutal truth. Saying "everything that happens to me is my responsibility". This is the part that is within our control, where we should begin our life encounter and see directly in the eyes of life, if our true intention and desire is to alter the pattern of occurrences and flip the circumstances into better side.

An "excuse" is a see-through belief that sticks to the mind firmly and has the ability to direct ideas, perceptions, and behaviour. We are unable to identify the excuse as it sees through directly into the justification in order to mitigate the responsibility and communicate to the brain that it is not my fault. The limiting opinions and excuses are not easy for us to give up as they are deeply engraved in our minds due to long-suffering, trauma and indoctrination, and we simply refuse to revisit and examine them and shift the responsibility to the government, parents, society, or God. The moment we realize that "something can be done", excuses evaporate like smoke.

Golden Cinderella

Fastest Women on Earth

June 23, 1940, St. Bethlehem, Tennessee, a girl was born fragile and premature in a very poor African American family. The 20th child out of 22 siblings. She was Wilma Rudolf. Only two and half years old when scarlet fever and double pneumonia struck her. 1944, at the age of four, diagnosed with polio. "When metal braces were put on my left leg, my doctors told me I would never walk again, and my mother told me I would, and I believed my mother", said Wilma. When her mother asked her, Wilma, what do you wish to be when you are older. Wilma replied, Mother, I want to be the fastest woman on earth. She continued her exercises and therapy. In 1952, at the age of twelve, she took her first step without the help of her braces. At the age of thirteen, she participated in her 1st school race and came last. She continued to come last in many more races to come. At the age of fifteen, she joined the State University of Tennessee and met her coach, Ed Temple. She said to her coach, "I want to be the fastest woman on earth". "With your spirit, no one can stop you", answered the coach.

1960 Rome Olympics, beyond the wild imagination of any mind, the world has witnessed lighting on the tracks, a sight to watch, an unstoppable speed wave flying like a falcon passing by its competitors, beating all the odds Wilma became "the fastest woman on Earth" winning not one, not two but three gold medals in one Olympics in 100-meter dash, 200-meter dash and 400-meter relay, the records being broken along the way by a paralytic girl who use to wear braces.

"I believe in me more than anything in this world." Wilma Rudolph

How many of us dare to have unshakable commitment and resolve to reach the pinnacle of life? I guess not many. Wilma has braces on her leg, but many of us have braces on our minds.

If our lives are not what we want, what excuses do we need to convince us that it is not our fault and we can't do anything about it?

The wiser we become, the more we are able to make a distinction between the real reasons of a situation and the excuses defending it; we are more prepared to acknowledge the ownership of our emotions and actions. Analyzing reasons helps us identify the area of our responsibility and points us towards the direction of the solution we're searching for and the action we could take. It also allows us to get above the need for justifications and make changes in our behaviour.

The supreme nature does not want us to be poor or keep suffering in a state of misery, but at the same time, the divine also does not like to give us charity and throw the abundance of riches in front of us. He wants you to uphold and maintain your self-esteem and self-respect and earn your right with dignity and honour through the skills, capabilities, intelligence, thoughts, capacity and crown of creations, the ability of making choices awarded to us to create our own circumstances as desired.

Accepting responsibility is immense power which can alter the conditions favorable in your life and to fully prepare you to overcome the perceived blocks, barriers, and obstacles that many people allow to hinder their progress by observing the world around them and allow the influence of others on them. That's the one factor that shapes their life experiences.

Understanding that your potential is not determined by external factors, such as people, institutions, governments, events, conditions, or circumstances. Your "True Power" is not determined by external factors unless you choose to allow them.

Taking responsibility for the current conditions in your life, regardless of what they may be, is a crucial initial step in becoming fully empowered to consciously and consistently create a life that aligns with your personal aspirations and start incredible transformations in your life.

Get up, go out to the universe and beat the odds up, remove the braces from the mind, you are being made partner in eternity because you are a divine thought with power of choice.

Over the course of history, societal standards were set to measure human status and worth. These standards are still in place and operative with full glory and might. Among these are the bloodlines, i.e the family someone is born in, the position or the status one is holding, the color of eyes, hair and the epidermis wrapped around the body, the profession and the most powerful power is the amount of money and wealth one has.

> **"Poverty is about low self-esteem and a lack of role models and opportunities. Without money, people resort to de-dignifying activities in order to support themselves. We free people through education and entrepreneurship. Freedom is self-determination, and you can't self-determine without understanding money and capitalism."**
>
> **(John Hope Bryant)**

Chapter 3
The Human Design

It is very important to understand how things and realities are created. Everything which is manifested in this world is initiated through a thought; that thought creates sensory desire, which triggers the action, and action creates consequential reality.

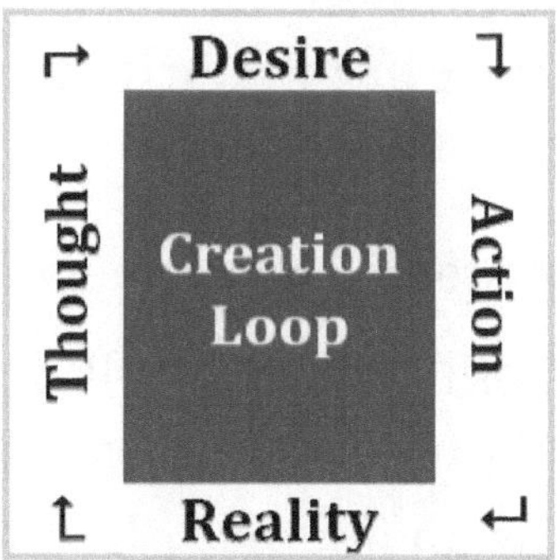

Thought stimulates a desire! (2) Desire triggers an action! (3) Action creates consequential reality!

There are six input channels which feeds information into the conscious mind which are sight, hearing, smell, taste, touch and thought. The information send by these channels is passed through an interpreter prism in mind creating an elaboration angle which augment, proliferate and rationalize the information based on the past experience.

The information imagery which is experienced by the person is an augmented, multiplied and rationalized perceived image as against the authentic and factual reality.

For example, appearances of people can be translated by the mind into perceived realities which could be entirely different from the factual realities based on the past experiences or indoctrinated information to the mind.

In a social experiment, one cold evening, a child left his mother and approached a huge tattooed biker wearing a black hoodie sitting on a bench in a park. He is perceived as an abductor by the mother based on his looks and appearance when she rushes to stop the child from reaching the man.

In another incident, a woman starts running, seeing a man chasing after her, shouting, "Wait! Wait! She reaches her house and locks the door behind her only to find the man saying Mam, you have dropped your wallet.

In a psychological study it is found that the better looking you are, the more people will deem you trustworthy even if they don't know you.

How thoughts are inculcated in minds in the early stages of life

A child, when opens their eyes to this world, starts assimilating the information spread around by the medium of six channels, which starts stacking in the subconscious mind in the form of thoughts reference folders.

These thoughts are generated and fed through the child's six receptors by the parents, teachers, relatives, media, literature, culture, clergy, society, scientific studies, etc. These thoughts keep adding and stacking in the subconscious mind folders throughout a person's entire life.

Through constant rhythmic retrieval process these thoughts are continuously rebooted and keep pouring non-stop on the canvas of conscious mind. Conscious mind, analyze, rationalize and synchronize these thoughts and settles them into sub-conscious mind's reference folders.

The quality and status of life are shaped around a person based on these synchronised thoughts.

We are now entering into a very core and crucial discussion on how the human mind works and how to put the intelligence and genius of the mind to work in order to create the circumstances of prosperity, wealth and happiness you want.

There are following six key components in the basic human design along with the three key attributes:

Six basic components of human design:

1. Soul (Non-Physical Infinite Energy Subsidiary)
2. Mind (Non-Physical Infinite Intelligence Subsidiary)
3. Thoughts (Non-Physical)
4. Emotions (Non-Physical)
5. Self-Mechanism (Non-Physical)
6. Body (Physical)

THE HUMAN DESIGN

As we see above, more than 80% of human being is formless. Any one of the components missing in the design will not constitute a human being.

"Human Design" integrates number of components to provide people insights into their own energetic composition and facilitate decision-making processes, and life purpose.

The human soul and mind are infinite subsidiaries of the prime source of the "Divine Supreme" and are directly connected to it to receive life energy and intelligence.

Since over 80% of human make-up is non-physical, humans cannot operate on a physical level alone, isolating themselves from their virtual reality and without taking input from the Divine eternal source of intelligence and energy. The crown of creations is the "power of choice", humans have to operate on both planes and discover their own individual purposes.

The reason why a definite and exact purpose is not disclosed to humans about their existence, and they are left to figure it out themselves, is due to their intellect, ability to make choices, evaluate outcomes and progress in the light of their experiences till they get there, and discover themselves their purpose and meaning of distinct life awarded to them. This entails the special status of freedom which humans have, to act and take independent decisions. Had the specific purpose been revealed to humans in advance, then they would also be following that purpose in the same manner as the other programmed creations. Humans are meant to be different and greater.

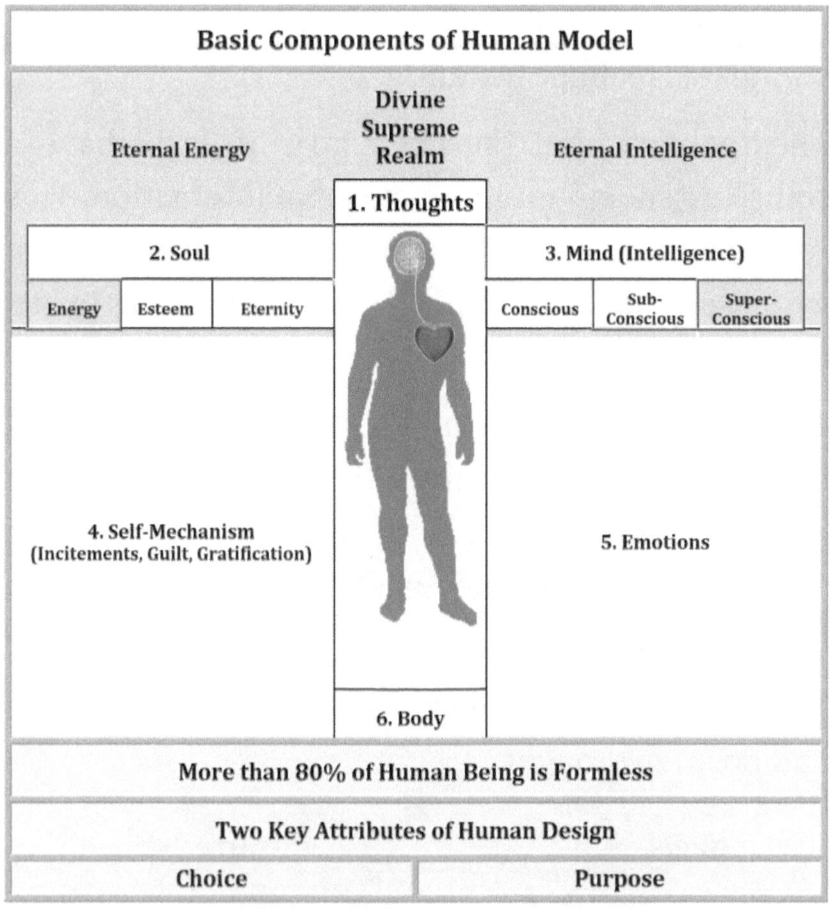

The body and mind operate together. Adverse thoughts and feelings influence the brain to release chemicals and fluids that instantly impair the performance of the body.

There are on average 60,000 thoughts reflect or pour on the canvas of the mind daily. Every time a thought lands on the canvas, mind releases chemicals which stimulates feelings instantly.

The thoughts and the chemistry of brain have a complicated and multidimensional interaction. This relationship can be influenced by a wide range of variables, such as our upbringing, experiences in life, and heredity.

The important thing to realize is that brain uses hormones or neurotransmitters. These are often referred to as chemical messengers used by nervous system to transmit messages between neurons to communicate thoughts.

The most common neurotransmitters for negative and positive thoughts are:

Negative		Positive	
Name	**Cause & Impact**	**Name**	**Cause & Impact**
Cortisol	Stress & Sadness	Dopamine	Motivation & Determination
		Serotonin	Mood & Confidence Stabilizer
Adrenaline	Fear & Anxiety	Oxytocin	Love & Trust
		Endorphin	Pain Reliever

Neuro Loops:

Thoughts and brain chemicals are reciprocal and mutually collaborative associations. The thoughts stimulate chemicals, and chemicals influences thoughts. For instance, stress releases cortisol and cortisol make you even more stressful. This creates a neuro loop which is difficult to break.

How to break negative loops and defeat negative thoughts.

A thought is an invitation to an emotion. Any anchor, environment, word, sight, face, picture, or past memory can trigger a thought and invite you to start the series of connecting events of thought consequence, fear, uncertainty, anger, anxiety, revenge or curse. Awareness is the key to identifying such invitations. Whenever you feel any anxiety, distress, hopelessness, or disappointment in a normal situation, always be alert and recognize it as Uh-Oh! Invitation has come. Refuse to receive or accept the invitation. Switch over to any happy thought, recollect any past achievement or change the environment. Switching over will suck the power out of the negative invitation. Always practice being aware and alert about these invitations and attack them back with the same rebellious response by making them feel worthless by not noticing them and ignoring them. This will make them feel worthless, powerless and humiliated. They will be shocked by your response, "Who are you?" as they have never seen such a response from you before. And when you overtake them, enjoy the victory & boost your mood. This is an ongoing battle; you have to learn and practice the art of awareness.

Brain Memory Disk (BMD)

Baby's heart, brain, and spinal cord start to form around week five. The central nervous system, which also includes the spinal cord and baby's brain. In the seventh week of pregnancy, the baby's spinal cord begins to form its first synapses. By week eight, the brain starts to fire electrical signals, enabling the kid to make the first unplanned movements, which medical professionals can even observe on an ultrasound!

The three main areas of a baby's brain, which starts functioning approximately after six weeks of conception in the fetus, are:

Cerebrum: This area of the brain is responsible for thinking, remembering, and feeling.

Cerebellum: The baby can move their arms and legs, among other things, since this area of the brain controls motor function.

Brain stem: The main function of the brain stem is to maintain bodily life.

The child's brain starts recording all of the thoughts and actions of the mother in the fetus. After birth, the brain keeps on recording the thoughts and actions you are performing during the rest of your life and continuously drives the results by interpreting and comparing these with past thoughts and actions, which influence your present life.

These cerebrum recordings can simply be illustrated as "Brain Memory Disk" (BMD). This is a storage house of your historical data of all your actions and thoughts in the subconscious mind, which stacks the information in memory folders and retrieves it consciously or unconsciously when a certain anchor is triggered and starts a series of interconnected automatic thoughts, negative or positive. The brain uses this data to help you make decisions in life based on your history of past experiences, social conditioning and indoctrinated belief systems.

The status and portrait of your current life is the reflection of what is recorded on your BMD, whether these thoughts are your own or transferred to you through your parents, peers or society which were accepted by you without resistance and rational analysis.

Since your present state of life is a reflection of your past BMD records, the future state of your life will reflect your present BMD thoughts, which are recorded there.

The is very important for you to have awareness of your human design and functioning of your life controlling device and what type of material is present on your BMD.

Awareness cannot erase your past data on BMD but can help to blur it to neutralize its effects on your current life and record the fresh information and beliefs on it for future landscape. BMD is not your foe; it is neutral in functioning and work according to what is programmed on it. You can reprogram it and it will become your greatest ally.

The enormous obstacle and massive challenge:

You want to change and decide to detach yourself from your old and transform yourself into your new one. That's the first major leap towards your success.

Secondly you need to watch your surroundings and associations with the people in your circle. The thought vibrations and energy fields of people associated with you affects your thought patterns and behavioral tendencies. Hence you must associate yourself with positive and optimistic people and distance yourself with pessimists and negative people.

It is found in numerous scientific studies that emotions and feelings are contagious and transmutable from one person to another. When you are dealing with pessimist people, you must endeavour to shield yourself with positivity, or else you may get burnt with the heat of their negative flames.

It is a long battle of your freedom. You need to know who is in control of yourself, your desire to be successful or your BMD. You need to take back the control from your BMD and must record the constructive information of your life on it consciously. You need to challenge at each step your powerful and equipped BMD who knows everything about you, your weaknesses, your strengths, your emotions and your experiences.

You have a desire to change your life and are taking actions towards it but fall into the BMD trap again and again influenced by negative attitudes from past. Don't get dejected or disappointed and hammer yourself. Admit that your BMD is all powerful and mighty in following the past patterns.

Keep activating and recharging your awareness, as it has been demonstrated time and again that beliefs do change, circumstances do alter, habits do get substituted, and negative tendencies do get replaced. This is the exact reason that choice, consciousness and intellect is built in the basic human design. If change had been impossible, then choice, consciousness, and intellect would have no meaning and purpose.

Not long ago, there were strong and unquestionable set of beliefs operating in human civilization, like:

- The belief that the world was flat,

- The belief that ships must be constructed of wood,

- The belief that contraptions heavier than air couldn't fly,

- The belief that the sound barrier couldn't be broken.

- The believe that the earth is placed on the back of a giant turtle.

Yet, in every instance, some brave soul was willing to risk humiliation to challenge the belief. And one by one, each belief was replaced by another belief.

Certainly, there is a tussle and struggle between BMD to do its duty and your desire to take back your self-esteem, make your life beautiful, successful and pleasurable in all areas. The capacity and valour of your desire decide your success.

As human being is the result of diving thought and master of his own destiny, it cannot remain the slave of its past.

When you are sleeping, the brain starts processing all the information, thoughts, experiences, and actions you have gone through throughout the day and stacks them in the BMD permanent data folders. Any new non-routine activity, attitude, behaviour or change in thought pattern gives an alert signal to the brain to decide whether to integrate it into permanent data folders or just ignore it. As there is no past reference point available in BMD, the brain simply places it on temporary memory. If this new behaviour and thought pattern keeps on repeating for four to six weeks continuously, the brain starts noticing it seriously and accepts to place it in a permanent memory folder. You need to talk to your brain about your transformed beliefs and positive thoughts, especially at the beginning and end of the day, just before closing and immediately after opening your eyes. The more lengthened and permanent your transformed thoughts and beliefs, the more deeply they become engraved in BMD.

The supremacy of the "Reticular Activating System" in changing behavioural patterns.

Are brain connections hardwired and unchangeable?

The traditional view which is been taught to us and made us to believe so long that the brain patterns which were developed in early childhood are hard wired and unchangeable. This means that if an undesirable, adverse, ugly, disgusting, unpleasant, horrible and objectionable pattern is once formed in our childhood, it would dictate and influence the rest of our lives, and there is nothing we can do about it except to suffer and live with it.

This is the same as once believing that the earth was resting on the turtle's back. If new learnings and experiences stimulate your brain to follow the newly acquired knowledge then your brain is not hard wired. It can create new connections to add into the total number of existing brain connections to grow and expand your brains' achieving capability and competence.

In our schools, in the science class, we were taught that there are two types of actions, voluntary and involuntary. Voluntary actions are the ones we perform intentionally and knowingly, while involuntary actions are not in our control and they happen automatically without us to have any time to think, like if we touch something hot, our brain automatically sends signals to withdraw our hand from the hot object. How this happens?

There is a special emergency mechanism which is independent of the Brain Memory Disc (BMD) and not controlled by the thoughts to function. It is called the "Reticular Activating System" (RAS) and is located in the non-cortex part of the brain at the backside. It works continuously non-stop and gets activated and takes control, interfering and freezing all the voluntary actions in exigencies.

For example, if driving a car, someone comes in front of it from nowhere, you immediately press the brakes. There is no time to think and act consciously, RAS will interrupt and freeze all other thoughts and actions you are doing and send order to apply brakes at that particular moment. Why this happens? Because your safety is on RAS's important list of priorities.

Do you remember, when you newly learnt to drive, you were very conscious of following the road signs and traffic signals and watching carefully others passing vehicles? After couple of years of driving now you don't even know or realize when you have reached your office, everything happens automatically without you consciously performing the driving functions.

How this transformation takes place from conscious actions to subconscious actions? The answer is repetition, you think and do the same thing again and again and it becomes the part of your belief system and get registered in RAS as something which is very important to you and it takes control and performs particular functions on your behalf.

Now, if I am able to drive this point successfully to you, then think if your thoughts and desires to change your life and become successful, respectable and prosperous are repeated again and again consciously in your mind, then these will be marked as something very important to you and ultimately get registered on your RAS important list. Every time you come across any information, experience, or impulse about success, respect, and prosperity, RAS will automatically send a message to the conscious mind to act accordingly towards that goal.

DOLLARS TO DIGNITY

Whether you are 8 years old or 80 years old, if you are able to register on RAS your belief that "you can", then RAS will destroy all your pattern of thoughts which say "I cannot" and form new connections. Note that the foundations of your beliefs are not based on the factual state of circumstances; it is your perception of reality that influences your beliefs. Your capability to achieve anything which you have decided to achieve is potentially unlimited. You can align your beliefs with the supremacy and power of RAS to change your only life you have on this earth.

> **I am of the opinion that my life belongs to the whole community and that as long as I live it is my privilege to do for it whatever I can. I want to be thoroughly used up when I die. For the harder I work, the more I live.**
>
> **I rejoice in life for its own sake.**
> **Life is no brief candle to me. It is a sort of splendid torch which I have got to hold up for the moment, and I want to make it burn as brightly as possible before handing it on to future generations.**
>
> **(George Bernard Shaw)**

PART 2

CREATE THE CIRCUMSTANCES YOU WANT

(Conscience & Happy Life Transformation)

Chapter 4

The Purpose and Meaning of Life

THE PURPOSE AND MEANING OF LIFE

What is the meaning of our life? Why we are here?

We might not know with accuracy the purpose of our life but there must be some, because without reason to live, to get up in the morning and make things happen doesn't make sense.

If, something happens in our life and we start thinking that life doesn't have any meaning, we just come here, we live and then die and it is all over.

I personally believe that we come from somewhere and we are going somewhere. We are not animals. We are human beings. We should enjoy the feeling of being human being. Divine has made us in the best possible design.

If you live, live in style. If you die, die in style.

Why are humans' superior creations? It is because of

awareness of being aware.

My every breath, every heartbeat, every pulse is saying that I am not useless and purposeless and created just to suffer.

Collective Purpose.

They say, life is a journey! But where are we heading to? What is our destination? Why are we travelling? Most people do not have answers to these questions.

We have been given talents, intellect, creative skills, and the power of choice to make decisions. But we don't know why? What is the purpose of all this? Some people try to find the answers in Ikigai and numerology, others in psychology, and some in theology.

Most of us are just experimenting with life and checking where life would take us. Remember, YOUR LIFE IS NOT A TRIAL VERSION! It is a onetime download real version.

There are two aspects of life. Individual and collective as the human race. If we reflect, then there must be two separate purposes, one at the specific individual level and the other at a common human level.

THE PURPOSE AND MEANING OF LIFE

1. Why humans were created among the other creations, and

2. Why are you created among humans?

Do you think that the vast cosmos system is established just for the sake of fun, without any meaning and purpose behind it?

Other than humans, all creations are just programed to do what they are supposed to do, going through their lives according to the instructions installed in them and they can't deviate from the that.

Humans are unique creations who are given the "power of choice" along with intellect and wisdom to make decisions, explore the meaning of life, understand the laws and functioning of this universe and apply this knowledge to the benefit of the creations.

In order to exercise the authority of "choice" there must be four fundamental conditions and prerequisites to be met.

1. **More than one option:** There must be more than one option available to choose from with varying degrees of results and outcomes. Without

options there is no meaning of giving choice to humans and it is as good as a "programmed human".

2. **Varied outcomes:** Options to choose from must have varied outcomes. If all the options have same type of outcomes either good or bad, then there is no point of giving choice. So, there must be different consequences of choices.

3. **Unknown Consequences:** Again, if the information of consequences is known in advance, there is no point of having choices as every time an option which is opted under normal and rational state of mind will always be the one with favorable outcome.

4. **Capability to err:** If the capability to err or make mistakes is absent, and only the correct decision is always taken, then the giving choice is pointless and illogical as without the capacity to error, the option with a favourable outcome will always be selected among others, which is as good as programmed selection.

Hence, the evaluation of choices and making decisions is left and trusted with human intellect and wisdom. Humans will surely err often and, pick bad options and get undesirable results. This is the process of knowing and learning from bad choices to be avoided next time. Here, intellect and experience become key strengths for humans.

This exceptional attribute of "choice" is granted to human creation is for a unique purpose. If humans were not created, that purpose would have not been fulfilled. All the appreciation and acknowledgement of the artist would have been programmed and under compulsion. Hence, there must be a creation who would have the level of consciousness to perceive the greatness of the art and the artist.

If a gem is to be evaluated, who would be best person qualified to do this, a blacksmith, a cobbler, or a gem expert. If the fossils to be studied, who would be the best person to give an opinion, a paleontologist (fossil scientist) or an economist.

The people who are qualified to appreciate the worth of a piece have acquired this expertise and knowledge over the period of time by studying, analyzing, testing, refining and improving based on the choices and not by force or under compulsion. I hope I am able to defog this point.

If you are with me so far, I would like to take you to the next thought level. Our original question was, as to why humans were created? We have discussed above that there must be a creation equipped with the qualities of choice, intellect and analyses to comprehend the universal artist and the art. But this was not enough. Human must be placed at a supreme position with the highest level of knowledge among the creations to make him eligible to access the artist and his artwork.

In order to have the highest position, he must have a unique laurel, which others do not have. That unique laurel is soul with three components, "Eternity, Energy and Esteem". Human Being was made partner in eternity, energy and esteem by installing the soul in him which granted him the supreme position above all creations.

If humans were not created this universe would be nothing else except an automated system of celestial movements with no one to appreciate and embrace its worth and value. Humans have given meaning and vibrancy to the robotic universe.

The more knowledge humans seek, the higher level of consciousness they ascend. More they ascend more closer view they get to comprehend the great grand scheme of the artist.

You are part of that great human idea. If you had not been born, would it matter to the great idea? Would it made any difference to the world? Would the Divine Kingdom have shattered, I would say yes! Had you not been important, you would not have been thought about. Divine thoughts are not insignificant, useless, purposeless and unimportant. Yes, the sun would not have risen if you had not been born; the winds, the rains, and the oceans would not be there if you were not born. Yes, you are required, and that's why you are here. You are an important component of the grand schema. If one component is removed from the system, the whole system comes to a halt and falls apart.

Individual Purpose.

What is your specific purpose in life as an individual?

At individual level, human beings are given certain in-born talents and capacity to acquire certain skills through learning and practicing. These talents and skills are applied in life to meet economic needs, self-satisfaction needs and to deliver benefits to the society.

The application of human talents and skills is a process through which the secrets of nature are unveiled, universal laws are discovered and unknown avenues of knowledge are found. In the process different products and services are produced and economic activity is generated along the way, which helps in contributing towards the benefit of humans and other creations.

The key question, however is where to use these talents and skills and how to find what we should be doing and why we should be doing. What is the actual purpose of an individual's life?

THE PURPOSE AND MEANING OF LIFE

To some people, it is very clear and straightforward; they know what their talents are and what they are born to do. For others it is a difficult and emotionally painful journey, they struggle sometimes their entire life to find the meaning and purpose of their existence.

This is quite understandable as life without meaning and purpose is like travelling a journey without any destination, shooting an arrow without any target, and living a life without knowing the objective, reason and meaning of what they are doing and why they are doing it.

The uncertainty, vagueness and fog in the mind creates the feeling of worthlessness and irrelevance and reduces a human to insignificant.

Let's make an attempt to find out the alignment between talents and economic roles through a small exercise leading to self-satisfaction and contribution to the society.

Make a spreadsheet of nine columns, as shown in table No.4.1 and fill in the columns and rows as per following description.

DOLLARS TO DIGNITY

S. No	Column	Description
1.	A	Write the serial number.
2.	B	List down your 10 key talents and skills aligned to your area of interest.
3.	C	Write three commercial activities in front of each skill.
4.	D	Add the % of earning potential from each activity. (You can use Google to have an estimation)
5.	E	Write why this cannot be done. ■ Write here against each activity all the obstacles and challenges, like regulatory restrictions, lack of resources, space limitations, lack of training, unskilled staff, etc.
6.	F	Write how this can be done. ■ Write here against each activity all the ideas, training, certifications, resources, reasons etc. which can make it happen.
7.	G	If your heart voice says: ■ "Yes" write = +1 ■ "No" write = -1 ■ "Neutral" write = 0
8.	H	If your mind's voice says: ■ "Yes" write = +1 ■ "No" write = -1 ■ "Neutral" write = 0
9	I	Write the total of columns G and H.

Take the highest totals in column I against each category. In the hypothetical example below, highest total is 3 against the categories of "Singing", "Public Speaking" and "Copywriting".

Let's analyze this a little deeper. Notice that:

In "Singing", the total of heart voice is +1 and the mind voice is +2

In "Public Speaking", the total of heart voice is +3 and mind voice is 0

In "Copywriting", the total heart voice is +2, and the mind voice is +1.

Note that heart voice will have precedence over mind voice and resonate more with the meaning and purpose of life at an emotional level.

In this example, "Public Speaking" is preferred over "Singing" and "Copywriting", although the total scores of all three are the same.

Within public speaking, there are three activities with the following scores:

Public Speaking Training Services with a score of 0

Keynote Speaking with a score of +1 and

Speechwriting services with a score of +2

A	B	C	D	G	H	I
S. No.	Talents/ Skills	Commercial Activities	Earning Potential %	Heart Voice (Yes = 1, No = -1 Neutral= 0)	Mind Voice (Yes = 1, No = -1 Neutral= 0)	Total
3.	Singing	■ Vocal Coaching	80%	+1	+1	+2
		■ Event Entertainment	70%	-1	0	-1
		■ Voiceover Production	80%	+1	+1	+2
		Total		+1	+2	+3
5.	Public Speaking	■ Public Speaking Training	70%	+1	-1	0
		■ Keynote Speaking	80%	+1	0	+1
		■ Speechwriting Services	70%	+1	+1	+2
		Total		+3	0	+3
9.	Copywriting	■ Copywriting Services	80%	+1	+1	+2
		■ Copywriting Courses	70%	0	+1	+1
		■ Copywriting Software	80%	+1	-1	0
		Total		+2	+1	+3

Hence, under "Speechwriting", the score is highest and equally distributed between heart and mind voice and perhaps the most plausible alignment with the purpose through which economic benefit and actualization could be attained.

You may try this with different areas of interest and skill sets till you hear the inner voice, ah, this is it.

DOLLARS TO DIGNITY

Hypothetical example for

INDIVIDUAL-SPECIFIC ECONOMIC AND			
A	B	C	D
S. No.	Talents/ Skills	Commercial Activities	Earning Potential %
1.	Painting	▪ Art Classes & Workshops ▪ Custom Art Services ▪ Art Supplies and Kits	70% 60% 80%
			Total
2.	Writing	▪ Content Creation ▪ Writing Courses ▪ Self-Publishing	80% 70% 50%
			Total
3.	Singing	▪ Vocal Coaching ▪ Event Entertainment ▪ Voiceover Production	80% 70% 80%
			Total
4.	Negotiating	▪ Negotiation Training ▪ Mediation Services ▪ Negotiation Tools	70% 60% 80%
			Total
5.	Public Speaking	▪ Public Speaking Training ▪ Keynote Speaking ▪ Speechwriting Services	70% 80% 70%
			Total
6.	Swimming	▪ Swimming Coaching ▪ Swim Gear Retail ▪ Swim Event Planning	60% 70% 60%
			Total
7.	Cooking	▪ Cooking Classes ▪ Meal Preparation/Delivery ▪ Cooking Equipment	70% 80% 70%
			Total
8.	Photography	▪ Photography Services ▪ Stock Photography ▪ Photography Training	70% 50% 70%
			Total
9.	Copywriting	▪ Copywriting Services ▪ Copywriting Courses ▪ Copywriting Software	80% 70% 80%
			Total
10.	Video Editing	▪ Video Editing Services ▪ Video Editing Courses ▪ Video Editing Software	70% 70% 90%
			Total

illustrative purposes only.

ACTUALIZATION PURPOSE MATRIX				
E	**F**	**G**	**H**	**I**
Why This cannot be done?	**How can this be done?**	**Heart Voice (Yes = 1, No = -1 Neutral= 0)**	**Mind Voice (Yes = 1, No = -1 Neutral= 0)**	**Total**
Write here against each activity all the obstacles and challenges, like regulatory restrictions, lack of resources, space limitations, lack of training, unskilled staff, etc.	Write here against each activity all the ideas, training, certifications, resources, reasons, etc., which can make it happen.	+1	+1	+2
		-1	-1	-2
		0	+1	+1
		0	**+1**	**+1**
		+1	+1	+2
		+1	+1	+2
		-1	-1	-2
		+1	**+1**	**+2**
		+1	+1	+2
		-1	0	-1
		+1	+1	+2
		+1	**+2**	**+3**
		+1	-1	0
		-1	-1	-2
		+1	+1	+2
		+1	**-1**	**0**
		+1	-1	0
		+1	0	+1
		+1	+1	+2
		+3	**0**	**+3**
		+1	-1	0
		+1	+1	+2
		-1	-1	-2
		+1	**-1**	**0**
		-1	-1	-2
		+1	+1	+2
		0	0	0
		0	**0**	**0**
		+1	+1	+2
		-1	-1	-2
		+1	+1	+2
		+1	**+1**	**+2**
		+1	+1	+2
		0	+1	+1
		+1	-1	0
		+2	**+1**	**+3**
		+1	+1	+2
		+1	0	+1
		-1	-1	-2
		+1	**0**	**+1**

Table 4.1

A life without the awareness of purpose and meaning is one of the major causes of low self-esteem and empty life. Efforts and struggle in self-discovery, purpose and knowing thyself are as crucial as your existence.

Living deliberately allows you to pursue your passions freely and to reap the material rewards and a sense of fulfillment and completeness that come with reaching your objectives.

Examining your personal identity and the concepts that underpin your beliefs and questions is the first step toward a truly happy existence. Who are you and what do you think?

Using your unique skills and abilities, lending a hand to others, and making a positive impact on the world—all while having fun and savouring every moment of it—are the cornerstones of Supremacy of Purpose.

There are no coincidences in your life. Things don't just happen to happen. Nothing outside of yourself has any influence over what transpires in your life.

It doesn't matter how awful your former experiences

were. Actually, it's critical that you let go of those ideas and focus on reaching your upcoming objectives.

You will then fully understand what it means to be living a purposeful life.

Genshai

Whether it is collective purpose of human creation or individual purpose, installation of esteem in human soul is divine feature to know thyself before knowing the artist.

I stumbled upon a book called Aspire by Kevin Hall, where I found an amazing concept about the meaning of life.

There is an ancient Hindi word called "Genshai" that means "Never treat a person in a manner that makes them feel small. Including yourself". What a great concept and meaning of life. Whatever our idea of life, whatever we do, whether collectively or individually, if at the awareness level, we treat people in a way that does not make them feel small and belittled. Will that fulfil your soul. Can that be your purpose in life? Can that lift your and others' self-esteem? If everyone practices this concept, can this World be a happy, peaceful and better place?

There is a law of polarization or dualism, which says that everything in the universe has two extreme opposites or duals which are same in essence varying in degrees. For example, on the polarity scale if we evaluate "light", the more we move the "light" towards the right of polarity scale the brighter the light would be. If we start moving it towards left side of the scale, the light will start getting dim and dimmer and ultimately the state of the absence of light would be called as darkness. It is essentially the opposite of the same thing varying to the extent of certain degrees between them.

Now consider this. Along with you there are other human beings who are by making bad choices moving the state of "happiness or pleasure" towards the left side of the polarity scale by creating situations through their actions and decisions, causing pain for other creations. How wonder full it would be a purpose of life to create situations through your ideas, thoughts, actions and decisions to move this state back towards the right side of the polarity scale. Will that satisfy the purpose of your existence? Will that give you a meaning in life? Will that make you realise the importance of your arrival into this world?

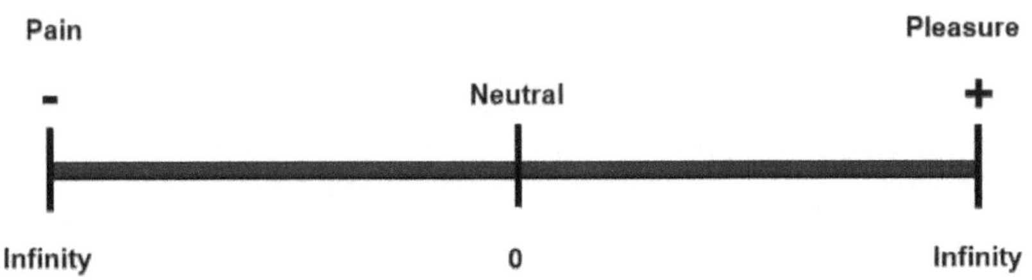

"No one is useless in this world who lightens the burdens of another."

(Charles Dickens)

Chapter 5

Mystery of Belief and Power of Thought

Belief the Result Creator

How we respond to an event is determined by our behaviour, which is dominated by our feelings and feelings are produced by our viewpoint. The painting on the canvas of our life is the reflection of our viewpoint. Our viewpoint creates feelings, and feelings affect how we behave in response to life events.

How are viewpoints created and cultivated? Viewpoints sprout from the beliefs we carry about anything, which creates feelings and drives our behaviour. The power of belief patterns is so magnanimous and enormous that they create a perceived realism around us that can be different from reality.

The practical demonstration of how the power of beliefs operates was first observed in the area of

Quantum Physics, a science which studies how and what in the visible and invisible universe is derived at atomic and sub-atomic levels, analyzing the things and tracing them back to their origin.

If we use reverse engineering and flip the process of thought conversion into physical form, we'll see the physical world in front of us, which is made up of matter. The basic unit of matter is called an atom, which is made up of three particles: protons, neutrons and electrons. The protons and neutrons are composed of quarks and sub-component of quarks are the particles called preons. The radius of a quark is smaller than 43 billion-billionth of a centimetre (0.43×10^{-16} cm). Smashing Physics by Jon Butterworth.

What we are trying to do is to use the established science to understand how everything we see around in our universe came into existence from the physical form which every one of us can see, feel and experience, backwards to its most basic form connecting it to the source which triggered the creation.

In 1905 when Einstein's incredibly famous discovery happened which is now known as $E=MC^2$

This is going to change the idea of the universe among the scientific circles as to what it is made up of. Einstein's discovery would prove that atoms could be broken into sub-atomic particles, which are packets of pure energy at the solid particle level. All the things in the universe, when broken down into their most basic form, consist of the same thing, which is energy. But the nature had a different plan to reveal the cosmic reality and educate us about the mechanisms of belief power.

So, what is beyond preons? As per Einstein, beyond preons is ENERGY.

Einstein's theory was soon to be challenged by another great soul in the arena of quantum physics from Copenhagen. Neil Bhor a Nobel Prize laureate based on his work with other scientists called "Copenhagen Interpretation" declared that the sub atomic particles were not particles but waves vibrating at different frequencies. Einstein and Bhor had many exchanges of views on this and later on it was established that energy initiates as waves and transmutes into particles based on accordant frequencies.

Bohr's discovery, in fact, divided the physicists into two groups. The one with the Einstein's' view of energy as "particle" and the other with Bohr's view of energy as "wave".

With the development of technology and accessibility of more sophisticated equipment, scientists were able to examine and test the sub-atomic state of energy more closely and with precision by the group of scientists from both the blocks, those who view energy as particles and others who view energy as a wave. The results of this research shocked the scientists when they observed that energy has dynamic behaviour and responds to the viewer and transmutes itself, appearing as particles or waves according to the individual thought of the scientist who was observing it. Meaning that it is the thinking of the scientist that would determine what energy would be converting itself according to the beliefs and thoughts of the person observing it.

This is the demonstration of the amazing power of belief in action operating at the thought level in the universe. **You see how your** belief systems and thought patterns influence your life and how you can transform your destiny based on your expectations, your thoughts and beliefs. Wave is a formless & virtual realm, and particle is a physical realm. The sequence of events that occur in this world is based on your thoughts. The thoughts are the creators of your life. A thought has given you birth, and thoughts shape your life.

Simply put that everything that exist in the whole universe is in its basic form is energy vibrating at certain frequencies which get attracted and get bonded with the energies of the same frequencies to form particles which we perceive as physical world.

"IN ESSENCE, WE ARE ALL THE SAME AND INTERCONNECTED".

Where Einstein Failed.

Mysteries of "belief" are endless and keep dropping the jaws of humanity every time you hear about them. If you believe a particular task is just a daily routine and ordinary and you can deal with them just as usual, your brain will prove to you that the task is just a routine and ordinary. Incredible example of the above is presented by Cynthia Kersey in her book Unstoppable about Geroge Dantzig a hard-working college student who study till late night and one day overslept and arrive late for the class. He noted down the two math equations written on the board supposing that these are tasks for homework. Initially, he struggled to solve these for a few days, but he was finally able to solve them and left them on his professor's table.

A sudden early morning call at six by his professor shattered his sleep. As George arrived late the other day for the class when he copied the equations from the board, he didn't hear the professor saying that the two equations on the board are unsolvable brainteasers for thousands of years and even Einstein wasn't able to solve these.

How was George Dantzig able to solve these? The reason is that in his mind, he was working on just routine, ordinary mathematical problems. This is the clandestine power of belief, if you believe that you can change your life, then you can. Just turn a deaf ear towards all the messages you receive that "you can't". Think success, abundance, wealth, prosperity and respect and you will achieve it. Think failure, lack, poverty and humiliation and you will get that as well.

If you look for someone who has already accomplished what you want to accomplish just follow the same actions until you achieve the same results. They say success leaves foot prints, take the same path following the foot prints till you reach your destination.

Nothing can prevent you from achieving the same outcomes as prosperous and successful people achieved. Your reality is determined by the emotions you attach to your beliefs. Belief is the creator of the factual reality. Your beliefs guide your thoughts and actions, if you remove the constraints and blocks of limiting beliefs from your mind, you'll experience the bright sunshine of success, happiness and prosperity reflecting on you.

Placebo Phenomenon

The amazing technology of "Placebo" has caught the attention of scientists in recent years, especially in the field of medicine. Placebo is a Latin word meaning "I shall please" It is a powerful coordinative impact of virtual belief on physical outcome.

Medical students during their studies discover that thoughts have an impact on physical body. It is observed that significant improvements appear in the patients who took sugar pills thinking that these are medicines. This is the effect of beliefs, called placebo influencing body, mood and attitudes.

Dr. Deepak Chopra presents a classic example of placebo belief in his book "How to Know GOD" that when he was a young physician, he heard about a patient who had fatal cancer and was essentially treated by an injection of ordinary, saline salt water. His body was entirely scarred by enlarged, cancerous lymph nodes when he arrived at the hospital.

This patient was frantic about receiving Krebiozen, the newest miracle remedy. His physician was appalled that he was wasting the medication on someone who would most likely pass away within the next week. However, he arranged for a single Krebiozen dose and administered it on a Friday out of sympathy. He went over the weekend, fully expecting to never see him again, but the patient was overjoyed to see him on Monday morning. All indications of the malignancy had disappeared; his lymph nodes were back to normal, and he was in perfect health. His doctor declared him cured, leaving him stunned even though he was fully aware that a single Krebiozen pill could not have conceivably made a difference in a few days.

However, a few days later, the patient learned that Krebiozen testing had been unsuccessful and ineffective. His cancer came back within a few days, and this time, he went into the hospital in a terminal position. With nothing more to offer, his doctor turned to the most extreme placebos. He lied to the client and said he would inject "new, improved" Krebiozen, but all he gave him was saline solution.

Once more, the man recovered in a few days. He left without showing any signs of malignancy in his body for the second time. However, tragedy happens when he later learns that the scientists have lost all hope in Krebiozen and abandoned all the research. The third time, he developed cancer lymph and died quickly this time.

The narrative's central idea, however, is that spirit operates by moving from the virtual to the quantum to the material plane. All miracles, whether or not they are associated with religion, share this characteristic.

The point to contemplate is, does virtual belief and physical reality talk to each other? Can a thought realm impact material realm? What is the connection between belief and placebo phenomenon?

Miracle Man.

The world has not seen before any greater exhibition of power of belief, which they have witnessed on May 6, 1954.

World sighted the absolute impossible becoming possible, the unattainable becoming attainable.

Before this date it was believed that humans cannot run a mile under four minutes and this belief was formed based on ground realities.

Physiologists and Doctors believe that any such attempt can lead to death.

Human bone structure is not compatible with the outcome; the wind resistance is the unbreakable barrier, and human lung power is inadequate. In ancient Olympic preparations, tigers were to be unleashed at the runners to increase their speed out of fear of life. Nothing worked in 6,000 years of history, till the date of May 6, 1954 arrived. Roger Bannister, a medical student, believed otherwise. "I believe I can do it; I have trust in my training and hard work, this is my reality and not a dream", said Bannister. On the Iffley Road track in Oxford, Bannister started running, "The earth seemed to move with me", he said, "I found a new source of power and beauty, a source I never knew existed." When the race ended, he touched the finishing line at 3:59:04 winning time and the history had been made. Impossible is achieved, 6000 years of beliefs shattered, bone structure become compatible, wind resistance is overcome, and human lung power is increased. Roger Bannister became the first man in human history to run a Miracle Mile in under four minutes.

He did not only break a 4-minute barrier but also broke the mental shackles of human belief. Once it is proved that humans can do it, the following month, just after 46 days, John Landy has broken the Miracle Mile. In one year further, 37 runners achieved the feat, and in 2 years, 300 people ran the 4-minute mile, and a few years later, 13 out of 13 participants achieved this. Now it is just a normal bench mark for the athletes.

This is how believes work they are contagious, they change the expectations, they set new possibilities, they change the paradigms of limitations. Once you prove you can do it, it opens the mental block for other to do the same and redefine what humans can achieve.

Humans believed they can fly and they did, humans believed they can sail on oceans and they did, from the heights of Everest to the depths of Mariana, human belief has demonstrated the possibility of impossibilities.

Like the historical limitation beliefs our individual belief system of limitations whispers us that we cannot do it as we are not designed to achieve. Our own beliefs are standing on the inferences of specific wind resistances and design structures. If you start breaking the legs of inferences one by one, the limiting belief will fall down and get replaced by empowered beliefs.

They say that, just wishful thinking cannot achieve anything; day dreaming and building castles in the air cannot bring any change in life. I say the life you see around you is actually built by the day dreamers and the castles builders in the air.

Edison's daydreaming of the incandescent light bulb has illuminated the world,

Martin Cooper's mobile phone craze connected the people,

Wright brothers' castles in the air enabled humanity to believe that they could fly, and they did.

The world around us is built and developed by the maniacs, crazy daydreamers and castle builders. Can you also see a dream for yourself to be prosperous, success full and respected in life? Is it a big ask? Can't it be achieved?

Power of thought

On one special moment back in eternity, a thought landed on the DIVINE canvas, igniting a desire to create creation; the rest is history, and the music of that thought is still going on.

Among billions of creations, the supreme divine had a thought, a thought which is going to manifest you into this universe. You are thought about for a particular reason; you are thought of because you can do something which others cannot; you can accomplish the job. Thought has fashioned you into the best design, the height and eloquence of creation, and the Miraj of conception. You could have been anything, like a rock, an animal, a tree, an insect, a bird, an amoeba or a bacterium. Instead, you are designed as a human. You are the masterpiece of divine thought. You were thought about because you are necessary; you are the announcement of the divine. You are HUMAN. Enjoy the feeling of being a human being.

MYSTERY OF BELIEF AND POWER OF THOUGHT

Understanding the process of how a thought converted into a physical universe is the real divine secret cognition of creation. What was the 1st cell, the building block, the key tool which is used by the Divine that brought physical universe into existence? The answer is "A THOUGHT".

Let's see the power of thought in human dominion. When Wright Brothers saw a bird and thought to create a contraption which is heavier than air and fly like a bird beating gravity, it was a crazy idea. When Martin Cooper announced that he was going to invent a device without any wire that you could use to talk to someone on a ship sailing over the water three thousand miles away in the ocean, "Send him to a mental hospital was the reaction". When Thomas Edison thought about the incandescent electric bulb, he was laughed at for the idea, when a thought came of having a device where you can see live events happening thousands of miles away, when it was thought about wheel, paper, printing press, compass, electricity, computers, internet, penicillin microwave, automobiles, it was all in imagination. The world around us was a thought at a point of time which manifested and came into physical existence and became a concrete reality in front of us.

Can you see, hear, smell, touch and taste a thought? No! So, are you denying that thoughts do not exist according to this measure of the existence of something? Of course, not as you experience the rain of thoughts pouring on your mind every minute and every second. They are real, they exist, and they operate at different levels of frequencies; good thoughts match the frequencies of good thoughts, bad thoughts match the frequencies of bad thoughts, and likewise, the thoughts of abundance match the frequencies of abundance, as they say, birds of a same feather flock together. Thoughts of the same frequencies vibrate and flock together and create the reality accordingly and determine the success or failure in one's life. Thoughts are the cause and the results are the effects of that cause. A thought when lands on the canvas of mind goes through incubation period and never get dissolve without creating an impact. Thought is the first cause and is the seed of creation, which transforms into reality and forms the existing physical universe according to the type of thoughts sown in mind. Like an orange seed does not grow into an apple tree, or a grass seed cannot produce an oak tree. If grass is sown, only grass will be reaped, and if mangoes are sown, apples cannot be plucked from the same tree. Similarly, lack, poverty, insecurity, fear, misery, and victimization thoughts cannot create an environment of abundance, happiness, security and prosperity around you. The good news is that by understanding this concept and divine law, thoughts can be altered, replaced, restructured and filtered to create the circumstances you want. Plant the right thoughts and get the right results.

So, as we have seen in the discussion of belief above, here is the revelation: Inferior thoughts communicate with other inferior thoughts at the energy level and create inferior life at the particle level in the physical realm. Whereas superior thoughts create a superior life.

If you have SUPREMACY OF THOUGHT over others, you'll experience supreme life.

"Belief bends reality."

Kinoko Nasu

Chapter 6

The Luck Design

Life and Luck Link

What is that common link in the process of creation between the Divine and you? The tool which the Divine used to create a physical universal empire was a "Thought" and the tool which you would have to use to create your physical universal empire is a "Thought".

Remember, thoughts are energy and they never die, they remain in the realm of divine universe. These "thoughts" signals which arrive on your mental canvas are transmitted from the massive universal "Divine Thought" pool to your mind. Human thoughts are usually not followed by the action and lack the intensity of desire to come into physical existence.

Thoughts that turn into reality provide control and power supremacy to the thinker and turn the flow of respect, tranquillity and prosperity towards him.

Do we have a control over our lives? Do we have capability to shape our lives as we want? Are our lives sailing on the "Sea of Luck" without any navigation wheel? Why one of our twin brothers is poor and the other is rich and affluent, is it just luck? We need to understand this whole thought, beliefs, creation process, before we discuss on how to use them to our advantage.

Before we go into the eye opening and mind-boggling discussion of "Thought" dynamics and "Physical Creation" and its relevance to the wealth and prosperity, let's understand briefly this mysterious factor called "LUCK Design" in our lives.

People often get perplexed and puzzled between a destined divine scheme and luck and mix up the two.

Destined Scheme is related to the divine plan on which you do not have any control nor you can alter it. For example, the moment of your birth was planned destiny and no one can change that moment.

On the other hand, luck arrives and knocks at your doors by invitation. Some people are considered highly lucky and others unlucky., they always seem to attract good luck or bad luck and this pattern remains the same throughout their lives. If luck is mere a chance or coincidence then there should not be any specific pattern of luck present in their lives, which indicate that luck follows the invitation.

Successful Lucky People

In studying the subject of luck, an interesting question always haunts the minds if we see the lives of successful people. Was Wilma lucky when she won three gold medals in the Rome Olympics? Was Roger Bannister lucky when he broke the 4-minute mile record? Was Edison lucky when he invented the light bulb? Was Harland Sander lucky when he spread his KFC empire across the globe? Was Helen Keller lucky when she won the Presidential Medal of Freedom and was elected to the Women's Hall of Fame?

Let me mention another lucky person, Soichiro Honda, founder of Honda Corporation, who was a poor student in 1938 with an ambition of designing ring pistons to sell to Toyota Corporation. In the morning, he goes to school, and at night, he works on his ring project. He spent all his little money and his wife's jewellery. After years of hard work at last he finalizes his design and took it to Toyota, who refused to buy. He went back to school, facing the mockery of his peers. He spent another two years improving the design, and this time, Toyota bought it. He now had to build a piston factory and needed material and concrete, but nothing was available as Japan was preparing for World War II. He and his friends collaborated and worked day and night to find a new method to prepare concrete, and finally, the factory was built. Ironically, during the war, the US bombed his factory, destroying it completely. Instead of being dejected, he directed his employees to collect the fuel tanks dropped by the planes to use this material to build the factory again. But this time, an earthquake flattened his factory, and he was forced to sell his operations to Toyota. After the war, there was destruction everywhere, resources were scarce and no gasoline was available for cars.

He found a small motor in his house, which he fixed in the bicycle to go to the market for groceries, and hence, the first motorbike was created. His friends saw this and asked him to do the same for them. Soon, the motors available at home were finished. He decided to manufacture his own and set up a factory. But again, there was a same challenge, money was not there. Instead of getting disappointed, he wrote to every bicycle shop owner about his idea, and out of eighteen thousand owners, three thousand agreed to invest. However, the bikes were not successful due to their size and heavy weight. Again, he changed his approach, refined the design and made it lighter. This time, they became a big success instantly, and Honda got the Emperor's Award.

Guess what, when people saw him, they remarked, how lucky he was to come up with this idea.

Today, Honda Corporation is one of the largest automobile manufacturers, with a workforce of over 100,000 employees. Same question again, was Soichiro Honda lucky?

Let's, briefly discuss the four types of luck operating in our lives.

Four Types of Luck

DIVINE LUCK

There is something which is called Divine Luck, you don't make any efforts, you don't use your talents and you don't even have basic elements and understanding of wealth and richness schema but you happen to be born in a family of a monarch. Now how is that! How can you beat 'em? The answer is that you can't beat them; they got a head start in life. It is the decision of the Divine. They might have deficiencies in some other areas of life, but in terms of wealth, richness and power, they enjoy absolute Divine Luck.

INHERENT LUCK

Again, there are some people who are not born into royal or rich families but still become wealthy and prosperous, like our rich twin brother who was born in a poor family, how this happens! They seem to have the natural ability and wealth cognizance inherently built-in and activated in them before sending them to the earth so that they can do wealth creation activities and make money-making decisions naturally, even without deliberate efforts, which seems impossible for others to do. This is called inherent luck, which the Divine has inherently activated in them. Why is it so? Is it just and fair? This is a topic that falls under the scope of another discussion. Maybe Divine wants to strike a balance between royals and the common man and create equilibrium and stability in the societies. It seems Divine wisdom understands that societies cannot function in extremely opposite situations of either everyone being Rich or everyone being Poor. So what should be the right mix and ratio, Divine decides on that, so we can't fight with that as well.

NATURAL LUCK

Now there are people who do not have a natural wisdom and wealth acumen built in them naturally, but they are not willing to submit to the pain of poverty and lack and are aware of the awareness that they have the ability to learn and change their adverse circumstances. They are lucky ones to have this awareness that they can turn the tables. This is what I termed as natural luck.

UNFORTUNATE LUCK

This may sound strange and absurd as how can there be unlucky or unfortunate luck? It seems self-contradictory and incongruous. I did this deliberately to drive the point home; if luck can be favourable and positive, it can also be unfavourable, unfortunate and negative. There are genuinely unlucky guys in this world those who are not aware that they are not aware that they have potential and capacity to struggle out their bad times and sufferings and change their gloomy and miserable financial state into abundance and prosperity. This failure to be aware is real bad luck, like an elephant that was tied to a chain in childhood. He is now grown up and has the strength to break the chain but is not aware of its own power and spends the rest of his life suffering in chains. There is not much difference between lower species and humans suffering from unfortunate luck, they are all in the same mental state.

The term "luck" describes situations or events that happen by accident, frequently with no obvious reason or source. It is frequently employed to characterize advantageous or positive results that occur suddenly or mysteriously. Luck is simply an inaccurate interpretation of how the universe functions. It's not something that we experience in isolation. The universe does not act through random incidences; it is governed by immutable laws. Happenings in your life are not coincidences or fluke of luck. As discussed in the chapter, human design, along with the physical body, also has a much larger energy field comprising of the soul and thoughts. Your body is limited by time and space, but your energy is unlimited and independent. When someone get an opportunity out of blue, meet a life changing person by chance, win a lottery ticket, just escaped death incident by missing a flight. The harmonized energy frequencies are felt and magnetized on the other side of the world. The thoughts and actions pull the opportunities that are pre-sought, the tickets are intended and pre-bought before matching the numerological attraction, going out to the society and circles where gravities occur among strangers. Strong positive thought frequencies repulse and throwback negative cosmic energies to escape incidents.

The thought energies of people sense and attract other harmonized energies no matter how far they are away from each other.

Self-talk that is negative can prevent you from reaching your objectives. Instead of letting negative thoughts consume you, confront them by finding evidence to the contrary or rephrasing them to fit a more optimistic narrative. Your thoughts are something you have created. Additionally, you always have the option to think thoughts that will bring you luck—thoughts that are empowering and positive.

If you are really interested in the deep study and understanding of this topic of luck, how it functions, on whom the goddess of luck showers her blessings and on whom it sprays curse, why do some people lead happy, successful lives while others face failure, can unlucky people do anything to improve their luck and lives and what are the four essentials' principals of luck, you may like to read the research book called "THE LUCK FACTOR" by Dr. Richard Wiseman.

"I've found great luck with three simple things:

A can-do mindset, tenacity, and intentionally surrounding myself with talented, high-character people who bring energy versus draining it."

(Andy Grolnick, chairman, security intelligence company)

PART 3

A WEALTH CREATION FRAMEWORK

(Successful Life Roadmap)

Chapter 7

The Supremacy of Passion

The Magic Word

124 years back, in the annual Super Bowl championship, Michigan finished the season losing to Penn and Wisconsin. The University's Head coach, Gustave Ferbert, resigned and left Michigan. In the turn of events, in the year 1900, Stanford University passed a resolution that only alumni would be the coaches of the university. Fielding H. Yost, the Stanford football coach who was not an alumnus, had to leave.

Michigan who was in search of a coach offered Fielding the position. Before joining Michigan, Fielding gave a media interview, claiming that Michigan would be undefeated in the next session and the combined scores of all the teams would be less than 49 points.

Michigan team protested loudly on Fielding's interview claim.

Fielding calls the team in the dressing room and asked them to remove their Jerseys and pile them up in the corner of the room. When you understand the meaning of this word, you can come and collect your shirts, till then you are not allowed to wear this color, he said.

A team that ranked fifth went on to become the Rose Bowl Champions with an unbeaten record of 11-0, outscoring their opponents by an incredible margin of 550-0 and becoming the national champions for the first time in history.

Michigan experienced a remarkable turnaround in 1901 igniting an offensive firestorm led Michigan to go four seasons undefeated streak, win 40 games in a row, and secure consecutive national championships in next four years. It took 5 years for the opponents to score 49 points.

Do you know what that magic "word" was, that Yost has asked Michigan to understand before they can retrieve their jerseys?

Whenever I asked this question in socials gatherings following the Michigan's story, I get the words like, endurance, self-belief, commitment, confidence, positivity, hard work, discipline, etc. These are all important traits, but the word that Feilding has asked the Michiganians to understand the meaning of was "Love". When they understand the meaning of love with the colour they wear and represent, they will put their heart and soul into the game to have unparalleled results. Fielding has injected a dose of passion into the players, which made them unbeatable.

This question is often asked, how do high achievers and performers keep going despite challenging and adverse circumstances and never stop? What drives them? The answer is "passion".

Passion is the energy infused into the willpower around which all other capabilities revolve and surrender to passion. Passion is an action mechanism for long-term endurance and battle. It is not a 100-meter dash, it is a marathon which keeps you going against all odds. Whenever there is a comparison between knowledge, talent and passion, passion beats them by miles. We have seen many knowledgeable, broke people; we have seen many talented people buried in the graveyards without leaving any impact on the world. But passionate people are the ones who have changed the world around us by keep going, failure after failure, defeat after defeat, and pain after pain. They keep the focus on the goal and never stop moving towards it whether creeping, sliding, small steps, walking or running, passion is the name of action.

Passion is a sun around which all other planets of attributes and components of success revolve.

The term "Passion" describes an idea that stands for tremendous zeal, passionate feelings, or a great dedication to a specific interest. Although the term has multiple interpretations, it typically refers to a symbolic depiction of the warmth, intensity, and energy that are linked with passion.

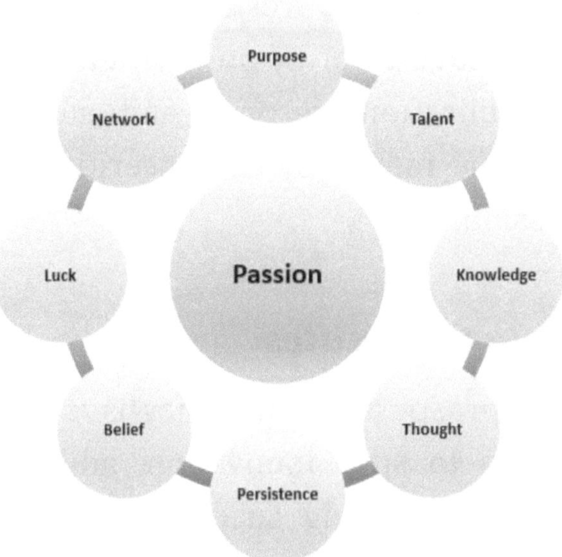

One way to conceptualize passion as a gravitational force is, as a strong, alluring force that pulls people towards their passions, objectives, or interests. Similar to how gravity draws items together, passion can draw people to pursuits or activities that pique their interest, motivation, and dedication. This allegory emphasizes how powerful and alluring passion is, implying that it has the ability to push people in the direction of things they genuinely care about, love, or are devoted to.

People are drawn to those who freely display their love for a given activity or subject because of the magnetic impact that results. Expressing one's passion can have a lot of positive effects, such as drawing admiration, respect, and support from people who are moved by the sincerity and fervour of that passion.

Passionate Corporates

A number of prosperous companies have successfully used passion to spur innovation, add value, and accomplish outstanding success. Here are a few noteworthy instances:

a) **Tom's Shoes:** Toms Shoes, a well-known example of a company that use passion to make a difference, was founded by Blake Mycoskie. Mycoskie saw a need for shoes in underdeveloped areas and developed a novel business plan in which a pair of shoes is donated to someone in need for each pair that is sold.

b) **Patagonia:** Well-known for its dedication to social and environmental problems, Patagonia has amassed a fervent following of clients who share their beliefs. The secret to the brand's success has been the founder's commitment to doing what he liked instead of just creating a business.

c) **Apple:** The company's love of design and innovation is responsible for much of its success. The company has distinguished itself in the tech sector with its emphasis on developing products that thrill customers and cultivate a strong work culture.

In addition to achieving financial success, these instances of individual enthusiasm, a drive to address pressing issues, and a dedication to a positive influence have left a lasting legacy for the communities they serve.

Karoly Takacs

Hungarian athlete Karoly Takacs overcome major obstacles to become one of the most inspirational figures in Olympic history. After military constraints first prevented him from competing in the 1936 Olympics, Takács suffered a devastating occurrence in 1938 when a grenade shattered his primary shooting hand, his right hand. He persisted and taught himself how to shoot with his left hand. Against all odds, he competed in the 1948 London Olympics and took home the gold in the rapid-fire pistol event. At the 1952 Summer Olympics in Helsinki, he replicated this accomplishment and made history by being the first shooter to win two gold medals with a non-dominant hand. Takács's tale is an example of tenacity, willpower, and the capacity to overcome suffering; his amazing accomplishments in the face of adversity and disappointments have inspired many.

In the realm of athletics, Karoly Takacs's narrative is extremely significant since it demonstrates fortitude, tenacity, and the capacity of the human spirit to triumph against hardship.

Takacs's story inspires people all around the world, showing that failure does not have to limit one's potential for achievement. His resilience, capacity to pick up a new skill in the face of adversity, and final victory at the pinnacle of competition are examples of the human spirit at its finest, showing how to overcome obstacles and go from tragedy to triumph by never giving up.

Why is passion such a strong motivator?

"An overwhelming passion is the final thought you think before you go to bed and the initial thought when you wake up in the morning," says Brian Schwartz, it feels like it has a hold on you, and you wouldn't be able to let it go even if someone asked you to stop. Devotion is sparked by passion!

Napoleon Hill investigated the wealthiest men in the world at the time in great detail. Their tales differed, but what distinguished them from common people was their unwavering dedication and passion to their goal.

"The soul has an obligation to follow its desires. It needs to give itself over to its supreme passion, says Rebecca West.

Albert Einstein, however, put it best when he declared, "I have no special talents." All I am is intensely curious. Imagine a brilliant mind such as that attributing his accomplishment to passion.

Because of the innovative concepts he used in his company, Richard Branson is a modern-day success story. And like many millionaires and billionaires worldwide, his current status is a result of his passion.

In a Stanford University commencement speech, Steve Jobs stated, "The only way to do great work is to love what you do." Continue searching if you haven't found it yet. Refuse to give up everything that concerns the heart; you'll know when you find it.

What role does passion play in leading a happy and abundant life? Everything! And I really do mean everything!

Whatever your passion is, it is an incredibly strong feeling that attracts to you the people, things, and situations you want to create because it generates favourable vibrational frequencies.

In what precise way does that occur?

You may easily think the thoughts that are consistent with achieving the desired result when you have a sincere enthusiasm for something. This, in turn, triggers the crucial emotions that will literally draw success to you.

When you consider the benefits that will result

from pursuing your passion, whatever it may be, the positive thoughts that flow from it creates a powerful vibratory frequency within you. As we've seen in the Laws of Vibration and Attraction, these thoughts along with the sensation or emotion of passion combines to create and broadcast a powerful vibrational frequency that, attracts the equivalent vibrating frequencies to create desirable results.

> **Nothing can take the place of passion.**
>
> **Talent will not; nothing is more common than unsuccessful men with talent.**
>
> **Genius will not; unrewarded genius is almost a proverb.**
>
> **Education will not; the world is full of educated derelicts.**
>
> **Passion and determination alone are omnipotent.**
>
> **(Calvin Coolidge)**

Chapter 8

The Dominance of Action

The most difficult thing is the decision to act, the rest is merely tenacity.

AMELIA EARHART

Action Activation Spectrum

The famous recipe of Colonel Harland Sandar of KFC was rejected 1,009 times by the restaurants. Howard Shults, CEO of Starbucks, was snubbed 200 times by the investors. Thomas Edison had to undergo 10,277 experiments to invent the incandescent light bulb. When asked by a reporter how did he feel failing more than 10,000 times before inventing the light bulb? "I have not failed. I have just found 10,000 ways that won't work, replied Edison. In all the above cases, it is the perfect reminder that failure or setbacks are not the end till you give up. Because they believed in the truth of their thought and the strength of their idea, they kept going till they reached their dream.

The action is the commencement of occurrences which baffles the mind and begins the process of bringing into reality the thought which was sown in the mind initially. It is now time to water and nurture that thought to grow into a giant tree. Actions move the mountains and take humans to the heights beyond imaginations of slothful dreamers. Action is the driving force, which lifts all the barriers limiting the human potential and capabilities.

Action must not be raw and blind. Execution of action must be built around four main characteristic questions. "What type?"," What time?", "What direction?" and "What intensity?". Knowledge of these four areas, translate the action into the desired results.

Knowledge is not mastery. Implementation is mastery. Implementation will win over knowledge every day of the week.

Success is in getting started. When you see someone successful around you, just recognize that he has started. It is the fear of failure which petrifies us to take action.

If you are trying to achieve a goal or milestone or trying to fix a problem in your life, applying action is the key component in making the things happen in your life.

Understand that Divine Supreme does not work on mediocre or average stuff. The human creation is a "marvel and masterpiece", and one of these creations is you, which is thought by the Divine Supreme. There is no such thing which is called average human being in an infinite universal realm. The results you get and the circumstances you experience is the outcome of the thoughts you breed, choices you make and the actions you take.

There is no such thing as an average manifestation; the process of attraction and creation is always a miracle, and the outcomes of each of these miracles have only been limited by your beliefs and labels based on your perceptions as to what you manifest.

If you choose poverty beliefs you align with poverty forces and if you choose wealth awareness beliefs you harmonize with wealth creation forces. In both cases the results are produced as per the choices you choose.

In essence, the design on your capability canvas is created as a boundless and unlimited creature. Activate the awareness of your intrinsic design and you will see the motion of big things start happening in your life.

The actions that are required to activate this awareness of your intrinsic divine design fall under the following spectrum:

Prime Responsibility	**Prime Thoughts**
Undesirable Thoughts	**Focus on the Target**

1. **Prime Responsibility:** If you will not take over the responsibility, you won't be able to take action to fix the circumstances. You need to understand that it is your responsibility to change your conditions.

2. **Prime Thoughts:** You must be aware of the thoughts that you think and start thinking

consciously about the thoughts that are required to believe that you are not an average person, you have the ability, and you'll do it.

3. **Undesirable Thoughts:** You should be aware of the undesirable thoughts and keep filtering these thoughts that land on your mind by instantly switching the focus to prime thoughts.

4. **Focus on the Target:** Your concentration should always be on the target you are aiming at, and you should not allow it to get off of your focus. You should keep adjusting your focus whenever your target gets out of focus.

It is entirely within your ability to understand and take the required steps to enable you to live a life of plenty, joy, and boundless blessings. If you make decision to regularly use these steps, the results will be overwhelmingly beneficial.

These behaviours have transformative effects of starting to achieve phenomenal results in your life by shifting the outmoded thinking process.

Action Barriers

Reading is easy, learning is easy, and taking action is difficult. If taking actions bear the desired results, then why don't people take action? Why taking action is so difficult? There are certain mental bottlenecks which block the desire to take actions and make it difficult to execute them, like:

1. Fear of failure

2. Action is uncomfortable as it requires to break the comfort zone

3. The purpose of the action is unclear

4. Absence of will to invest time, energy and commitment.

5. Non-availability of a "system" to follow.

"If we don't like what's happening to us in the world, all we have to do is change our consciousness -- and the world out-there changes for us!"

(Lester Levenson)

THE DOMINANCE OF ACTION

Why many people are not successful?

Because of FEAR!

Albert Camus, a famous author and philosopher. He named the 17th century as the century of math, the 18th was the century of physics, the 19th was the century of biology. Then, he shocked the public by naming the 20th century the century of FEAR.

Ann Landers was once asked, what is the most dominant problem in people's lives?"

"It's fear!" she replied. "People live in bondage with their fear. They're afraid of losing their wealth. They're afraid of losing their loved ones. They're afraid of being themselves. They're afraid of growing up and being responsible. **They're afraid of life itself!"**

Fear stems from the unseen, uncertainty and lack of knowledge. Put down all possibilities that can go wrong on paper and prepare a strategy to mitigate them. Have your alternate course of action ready if this happens or if that happens. This will help anticipate the outcomes and prepare counter plans in advance to deal with unfavourable circumstances.

The fact is that the real action pulls us out of our

comfort zones. It demands purposeful time and effort.

Why we need to achieve something, we are unclear of its purpose. Our desire is weak, our "why" is meagre, we are not prepared to invest time, efforts and energy to it.

We do not have any system or a model to follow or any strategy to start with.

We do not comprehend that the mind is the vehicle and the heart is the fuel. Mind thinks a plan, and the heart provides the emotional fuel to take action. We need emotions to feel our painful and disgusting current circumstances, which require passionate action to drive us out of these circumstances. Without passion and execution, brilliant and intellectual ideas finally get buried in the cemetery.

We need to ask these questions to ourselves if we want to get somewhere in life:

1. How will we feel emotionally if we achieve this particular goal (Whether health or Wealth)?

2. Who are you without this goal? What is your identity and self-worth?

3. How will it affect your family and other people if this goal is not achieved?

4. If you had accomplished this goal five years back, what openings would have been available to you today?

Manifest your aspirations into reality pursuing your genuine desires need more than mere wishful thinking. It entails constructing a systematic approach to transform ambitious objectives into manageable tasks. Reading all the books on swimming in the world will not make you swim until you get into the water. The biggest obstacle in taking action is "FEAR".

A young novice swimmer who was scared of jumping into the water surrounded by experienced swimmers was encouraged to jump as he looked really afraid, and accidentally shoved off the board. Guess what happened the next moment, "Fear" vanquished as a result.

This explains one key lesson that taking action dispels fear, hesitancy, and indecision, nurtures fear and magnifies the anxiety.

100 great concepts and ideas, abandoned or pending, are unimportant against one good idea developed and implemented. Nothing is produced or created just by thinking, from needles to skyscrapers, from bicycles to space shuttles, until the idea is put into action.

Many great ideas went to the grave as they were on hold for acting upon till every circumstance was completely favourable. The yearning to be perfect is desirable; however, in this world, there is nothing which is created by humans that is perfect and flawless and does not have room for improvement, nor will it ever be. Waiting for ideal circumstances is waiting forever.

Engrave this on your heart, "No matter how brilliant the idea is, you will gain nothing unless you act upon it". The saddest and most painful words in your life would be "Had I taken this decision some years back, the life would have been so much meaningful. I regret not taking action when I had to."

By taking action, have you deliberately crafted your future? The decision is pending with you.

THE DOMINANCE OF ACTION

You now have realized the importance of taking action, but what is next? These four broad questions above are meant to put you on the correct path to being more action-oriented, regardless of what you've been studying or trying to achieve.

Are you prepared to take action?

There's a reason why so many individuals still find it difficult to apply the abundance of knowledge that is currently available to real and practical actions. The fact is that taking action demands far more willpower and motivation than just reading stuff and not applying it.

"Action is the foundational key to all success."

Pablo Picasso

The formula is simple: action = change = success.

These are the three desires people hesitate to discuss in public!

1. A desire to develop consistent income streams

2. A desire to develop self-esteem and a confident personality and

3. A desire to find a purpose and meaning in life

The solution to these desires is crucial and must be instantly implemented because:

The Biggest Problem in Life

The biggest problem in life is that TIME is running out! (In fact, Life is running out). Why do we always wait to lie on the DEATH BED to understand the wisdom and the purpose of our life? Why we always decide to do something meaningful in life when there is no tomorrow left with us?

The important news is that right now, there are still lots of "Tomorrows" left with YOU!

That one action, yes, just that one action, can make all the difference.

People are professional "victims."

How many times did you think about attempting something and consider not doing it because you thought you would fail or cannot be successful because someone told you?

It is a mindset. When I change my mind set. A horrible thing happens. I can't blame society, government, people, friends, circumstances, luck or Divine anymore for my failures and miseries.

This was frightening in the beginning but gives strength & Freedom to think ultimately.

To change mindset, it needs only one second. But for many that one second comes when there is no tomorrow left.

Why don't we change our mind set NOW when there are still many tomorrows left?

> **"If you don't want to have regrets later, then now is the time to take action, not tomorrow, not next year, not when you feel like it, not when it's convenient—now is the time to take action."**
>
> **(Joyce Meyer)**

Chapter 9

The Wealth Creation - Introduction

THE WEALTH CREATION - INTRODUCTION

"Climb the hills of wealth through the skills of wealth"

Wealth Creation is one of the most significant, delicate, and fascinating topics in the human history, yet sadly, it is not taught in schools or colleges and is generally disregarded. Taking advantage of this, the world has witnessed the largest frauds, money games, Jack Pot lotteries, gambling, high-return investment opportunities, illicit mutual fund schemes, etc., at their peak in recent years, which reflects people's sincere desire to become wealthy as quickly as possible with little to no work. The average middle-class person is continuously suffering at the hands of the exploiters due to the constant traps since they are well aware of human psychology.

We will go into great length on this topic using just logical arguments in order to clarify the fundamental ideas behind creating riches without delving into immoral, unlawful, or fraudulent money-making schemes.

The big question is, how to make lot of money? The short answer is, "Sell". Became terrified! In reality, though, there isn't any other option.

Some would say, "I work at a job and I make good money without selling," Job Oh yes! Indeed! Do you recall the day of the interview when you convinced your interviewer that he was sold on your selling skills and that you were the best person to hire?

Do you still detest the term "selling"? Okay, then swap it with "persuasion"; this may settle the flow of adrenaline in the body.

Selling is everything in life. Suppose you have an idea you have to have skills to buy people into it. If you are looking for a job, you have to sell your skills to the interviewer to hire you. If you are married, then you are already a biggest salesman, who has successfully sold the idea to your partner that you are the best person to live with rest of your life.

It's crucial to understand that selling is a necessary component of wealth creation in life. Gaining confidence, reframing negative selling impressions, and honing sales techniques can all help people get over their concerns and become more successful in life. It would be rewarding if you view selling as an opportunity to help others by putting an emphasis on adding value, developing relationships, and actually assisting people in solving their problems.

Three Legal Ways of Having Money and Wealth			
1	**2**	**3**	
Through Self Efforts	Through Leveraging Wealth	Without Efforts	
Selling of Idea, Skill, Product, Service	Money, Property, Gold, Bonds, Stock, Crypto, Interest	Donation, Aid, Charity, Alms, Gift, Lottery	Born in Rich Family (Inheritance)

Although our body houses our mind, it is our mind that governs our body, yes, we have lack of skills, we fear the thought of acquiring certain skills. Yes, we have flaws and we will never be flawless, but it is our responsibility to recognize our flaws, work towards fixing them, learn the skills required to change and improve our lives and strive for perfection.

Four Types of People

From the perspective of richness and prosperity, there are four types of people in the world:

DOLLARS TO DIGNITY

Peoples Wealth and Wisdom Matrix					
Type 1	They have wealth	And	They have wisdom	Ultra-Rich	Positioned at the best point of humanity
Type 2	They do not have wealth	But	They have wisdom	Unwealthy	
Type 3	They have wealth	But	They do not have wisdom	Filthy Rich	Positioned at the worst point of humanity
Type 4	They do not have wealth	And	They do not have wisdom	Dirt-Poor	

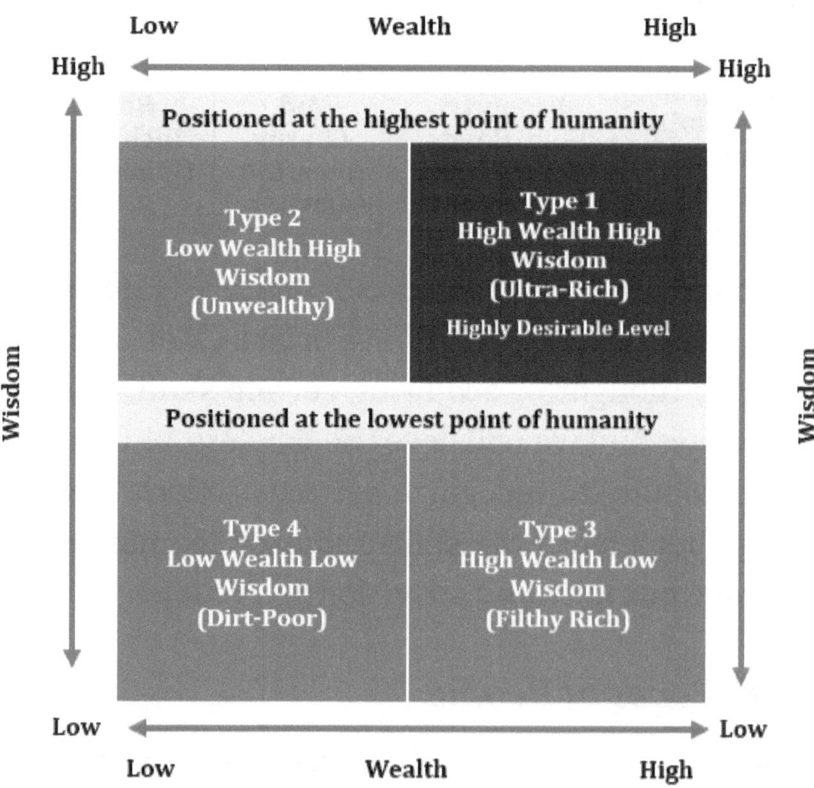

Type 1 People: These are the people who have wealth and wisdom. They use their money wisely, they have high self-esteem, they do not like the display or show off of their wealth. They have compassion and mercy for others and they contribute towards the betterment of society and help people. They are ultra-rich people and are positioned at the best point of humanity.

Type 2 People: These are the people who do not have wealth but have wisdom. They have compassion and mercy for others and have desire to help underprivileged people like Type 1. that they too, would contribute towards the betterment of society if they had wealth. They are rich in wisdom but are unwealthy and are also positioned at the best point of humanity.

Type 3 People: These are the people who have wealth but do not have wisdom. They use their money unwisely; they have low self-esteem, and they like to display and show off their wealth. They do not have compassion and mercy for others, and they do not contribute to the betterment of society or help people. They are filthy-rich people and are positioned at the worst point of humanity.

Type 4 People: These are the people who do not have wealth and do not have wisdom. They have low self-esteem, and have desire to be wealthy like Type 3. They also would like to display and show off, if they had wealth. They do not have compassion and mercy for others. They are dirt-poor people and are positioned at the worst point of humanity.

Poverty is inhuman, insulting, disrespectful and disgraceful to humanity, devilish, criminal and worse than cancer and aids. Poverty is man-made, and so is richness. Society looks down upon the poor.

Employment and jobs are drying up, and skills are getting redundant at a fast pace.

There are two biggest problems in life:

1. Time is unstoppable and is running out.
2. The time zone ahead (Future) is unseen and uncertain.

We do not know what future holds for us. If life is predestined and pre-written then decision making and unseen future becomes irrelevant. The only way to predict future, precisely and accurately is through laws of nature, which are irrefutable and gives the same result always. You apply the law and you know the result.

Why rich are always rich and poor are always poor? If rich become poor by accident or any bad decision, they become rich again soon. If poor become rich by chance or accident, they become poor soon. Why?

The secret lies in this answer: "Types of thoughts". We have discussed this in length above. Poverty attracts poverty and richness attracts richness. Rich do not associate themselves with poor to lose their wealth and poor do not associate with rich to increase their wealth.

What is the solution to this dilemma? First, change your thoughts. Stop putting wrong things in mind, "Constant Negative News (CNN)". Start putting the right things. Second, use the power of leverage. Combine your small contributions to make it equal to the pool of the rich and increase your wealth. Every one of you should be a master salesman.

You also need to know yourself and what are you selling before anyone else does. Be aware of your advantages and disadvantages, how you come across in a professional setting, and the value you bring to the lives of the people. To close any knowledge and skill gaps you may have in starting your business venture, you may need to associate and form alliances with other people. Nobody has ever created a profitable company by themselves!

Basic Wealth Building Blocks

Following are the nine basic wealth building blocks, which can be the starting point towards the wealth creation process.

1. Purpose

2. Problem

3. Solution

4. Market Road Map

5. Traditions and Trends

6. Unique Niche

7. System

8. Leverage

9. Luck

THE WEALTH CREATION - INTRODUCTION

The ambitious people with clever business sense and credibility see deep through these basic points, a huge potential, and build upon it the financial fortresses around themselves and their generations and enjoys the power and freedom which many dream of. We will discuss each of these points now.

Basic Wealth Building Blocks to Start With

ORCHESTRATING

1. Purpose	2. Problem	3. Solutions
a) Self Esteem b) Type 1 (Ultra-Rich)	a) Problems of people b) Market issues	a) Tailored solutions

RESEARCHING

4. Market Road Map	5. Tradition/Trends	6. Unique Niche
a) Knowing the market b) Demand Analysis c) Data Analysis	a) Product b) Service c) Skill d) Idea	a) Macro Level b) Micro Level c) Nano Level

IMPLEMENTATION

7. System	8. Leverage	9. Luck
a) Sales Funnel b) Delivery Channels	a) Belief d) Action b) Passion e) Branding c) Desire f) Network	a) Natural

> **"Energy and imagination are the springboards to wealth creation."**
>
> **(Brian Tracy)**

Chapter 10

The Wealth Creation - Orchestrating

Basic Wealth Building Blocks to Start With		
ORCHESTRATING		
1. Purpose	2. Problem	3. Solutions
a) Self Esteem b) Type 1 (Ultra-Rich)	a) Problems of people b) Market issues	a) Tailored solutions

Purpose

Being prosperous is much more than just acquiring wealth and tangible belongings. A feeling of purpose in life, robust relationships, good health, and the ability to live life on your terms are all indicators of true prosperity. Money brings freedom, security, and the capacity to lend a hand to others. It enables people to get rid of tedious tasks, take breaks, and follow their passions. Additionally, wealth can provide advantages and positions in social, political, and legal spheres. The ultimate goals of wealth are to achieve financial independence, have a stress-free retirement, practice philanthropy, take care of one's family, travel, and create memorable experiences that add to a happy and meaningful life.

There are two aspects of having the purpose of wealth in your life:

First, you need to keep this always in mind as to why you want to be wealthy and have an abundant and prosperous life. We have seen that one of the important components of the soul is "Esteem". It is your soul's right to be respected and have esteem. You do not want the control of your life to be in the hands of others just because you lack the resources to meet your economic needs.

Second, as you value and protect your self-esteem, you feel compassion towards others and want to contribute towards the betterment of society and help people. You would like to be in Type 1 category of ultra-rich to be standing at the best point of humanity.

When you keep the above two purposes in front of you, you will be able to overcome all the obstacles and challenges that come your way in the journey of wealth creation. It will keep your passion ignited and give you the energy and meaning to keep going.

Problems

You need to map the problems and inconvenience people are facing in any particular area of their life with the products, services or the ideas you would like to develop for them.

When attempting to address issues in the market, businesses may encounter the following difficulties:

Not Knowing How to Explain the Goods or Services: Companies may find it difficult to convince prospective clients of the worth and advantages of their goods or services. This problem occurs when there's a mismatch between what company provides and what customers want.

Not Finding the Correct Market Segment: It can be difficult for firms to pinpoint and identify their ideal clientele. Without a thorough grasp of their target market, companies could find it difficult to successfully customize their goods or services to fit the needs of certain clients.

These difficulties draw attention to how crucial it is to have clear communication, comprehend client categories, and coordinate sales and marketing initiatives.

It's critical to have a deep understanding of market issues in order to evaluate consumer problems and create products and services that address those needs. Following steps can help to determine the problems and issues customers are facing.

Recognize Market Issues: Begin by gaining a thorough understanding of your target market's problems, annoyances, and unfulfilled demands. This entails expanding your consumer base to include prospective clients as well as non-clients.

Differentiating Issues from Wants: Make a distinction between issues facing the market and consumer preferences or rivalry. Problems are tangible, quantifiable, and the main factor influencing a customer's decision to buy a product.

Apply the "Jobs-to-be-Done" Theory: The term "jobs to be done" (JTBD) describes a framework, theory, and viewpoint in business that explains why consumers purchase goods.

According to the jobs-to-be-done theory, often known as the job's theory, consumers "hire" things to do tasks like satisfying desires or finding solutions to problems rather than purchasing them. This theory highlights the idea that people purchase goods in order to advance in their life. Knowing what motivates consumers to purchase a product or not might help you pinpoint market issues efficiently.

Conduct Customer Interviews: To learn more about the issues, requirements, and preferences of current and prospective consumers, conduct interviews with them. Look for trends in the comments to determine prevalent issues in the market.

Perform Surveys: To verify the widespread nature of the identified market issues, surveys should be performed using the information obtained from interviews. Utilizing surveys to gauge the prevalence of these problems within your target market

This process can provide a greater understanding of developing the product and services and can offer important insights into the issues that the target market is facing. This will help to create goods and services that satisfy consumers and successfully fulfil market needs.

Solutions

Creative solutions to clients' issues entail a client-centric strategy that prioritizes successfully meeting their demands. Here are a few creative approaches to resolving client issues:

To design solutions to the problems of people while developing products and services for them, it is essential to follow a structured approach that involves understanding market problems thoroughly and aligning solutions with customer needs.

Position Yourself as a Problem-Solver: Embrace your role as a strategic designer or product developer by focusing on solving bigger problems for your clients. Position yourself as a problem-solver rather than just a creator of deliverables to stand out in a crowded market.

Create Tailored Solutions: Tailor your design packages and messaging to emphasize your problem-solving capabilities. Showcase your commitment to solving problems and creating impactful solutions for your clients.

Empathy and Active Listening: By learning about customers' problems and paying attention to what they have to say, businesses can come up with creative solutions that are customized to meet their unique requirements. Businesses may create solutions that resonate with their target audience by genuinely understanding their difficulties and having empathy for customers.

Continuous Improvement: Businesses should upgrade their products or services on a regular basis in response to input from customers and shifting market expectations. Businesses may create innovative solutions to meet the needs of their clients by remaining flexible and attentive to their demands.

Customer-Driven Innovation: You can stimulate customer-driven innovation by interacting with reviews, comments, and suggestions from customers. Businesses may produce products that directly address the needs and preferences of their customers by paying attention to what they have to say and implementing their suggestions into the process.

Unique Value Propositions: The secret to creatively resolving client issues is to offer distinctive solutions that set a product or service apart from rivals. Emphasizing the advantages and worth that clients will obtain can draw in more business and distinguish a company in the industry.

Here are a few instances of creative fixes for client issues:

Netflix: By offering a subscription-based streaming service that enables customers to watch a sizable collection of films and TV series on a variety of devices, Netflix transformed the entertainment sector.

This creative solution upended conventional cable and satellite television, improving customer experiences and offering a convenient way to access entertainment content.

Uber: Uber revolutionized the transportation sector by launching a practical and effective ride-sharing service via a mobile app.

This creative idea revolutionized the way consumers hail cars, having a big influence on established taxi services and giving drivers in the gig economy various earning options.

Amazon Prime: This subscription service provides advantages, including quick shipping, easy access to a huge selection of films and TV series, and exclusive offers on Amazon's online store. Combining different services into one bundle increases customer loyalty, boosts revenue, and gives customers a complete package that adds a lot of value to their membership.

These illustrations highlight how creative solutions may improve customer experiences, solve problems for customers, and raise the general calibre and value of services across a range of industries.

> **"The single most powerful asset
> we have is our mind. If trained well,
> it can create enormous wealth."**
>
> **(Robert Kiyosaki)**

Chapter 11

The Wealth Creation – Researching

Basic Wealth Building Blocks to Start With		
RESEARCHING		
4. Market Road Map	**5. Tradition/Trends**	**6. Unique Niche**
a) Knowing the market b) Demand Analysis c) Data Analysis	a) Product b) Service c) Skill d) Idea	a) Macro Level b) Micro Level c) Nano Level

Market Road Map

A market study that examines a certain market in-depth to be conducted to see whether it is viable for a given commodity or service. It entails examining a number of variables that affects the customers demand.

Comprehending the Market:

Target Market: A certain customer segment that is most likely to be interested in the specific product or service is the focus of the study. It explores their purchasing patterns, needs, wants, and demographics.

Competition: The research examines the products, services, advantages, disadvantages, and market share of the current competitors in the industry.

Market trends: It pinpoints new and developing patterns that may have an effect on the expansion or contraction of the market. This covers changes in the social or cultural sphere, the economy, and technology breakthroughs.

Analysis of Consumer Demand:

Product/Service Fit: The study evaluates how well the suggested good or service fits the target market's requirements and preferences.

Pricing Strategy: It examines variables, including production costs, rival pricing, and customer willingness to pay, that affect pricing decisions.

Distribution Channels: Using retail outlets, internet platforms, direct sales, and other channels, the study investigates the most efficient ways to reach the target market.

Collecting and Analyzing Data:

Methods of Market Research: A combination of primary and secondary research methods may be used in this study. Primary research includes gathering information directly from prospective clients via focus groups, interviews, or surveys. Collecting pre-existing data from government statistics, industry journals, and market research reports is known as secondary research.

Data analysis: In order to find patterns, trends, and insights that guide decision-making, the gathered data is examined.

Results and Utilization:

Go/No-Go Decision: In light of the results, you may choose to proceed with the product or service launch or modify your strategy in the light of the market's insights.

Development of Marketing Strategies:

The research helps create marketing plans that will position the product or service, reach the target market, and increase sales.

Resource Allocation: Businesses can more effectively allocate resources for sales, marketing campaigns, and product development as a result of the findings.

A market study is essentially a road map that helps companies negotiate the intricacies of a given market and decide on product development, marketing, and overall business strategy.

Tradition and Trends

Timing the trends.

There are people who are making money because of the trends and there are people who are losing money because of the trends. The people who are making money are those who are in front of large trends and people who are losing money are those who disregard trends.

How do you get in front of large trends? Study what creates those trends. If you are successful today, it doesn't mean that you will going to be there forever. Every year, you have to work harder to earn the same amount of money. An important principle is to focus on the product and service categories that are huge and expanding.

What happens to the vinyl record industry? In 1985, it was a booming two billion dollar a year business. By 1990 – just 5 years later –this industry was eliminated off the face of the earth due to its short vision, which couldn't see the coming revolution of Compact Discs.

What are the latest trends? Health? Retirement concerns? Life and wealth Security? New Technologies - E-Commerce/Internet- Artificial Intelligence?

Whatever it is you have to keep your eyes, ears and mind open to understand the mood of people, what is happening around you, where the world is heading and what are the current trends.

Products and services should strike a balance between tradition and trends to ensure long-term success and growth. While traditional practices provide a strong foundation for a business, incorporating trend-focused approaches can bring new opportunities for innovation and differentiation. Traditional methods, such as a strong emphasis on customer service and quality, can lead to customer loyalty and positive word-of-mouth marketing.

On the other hand, integrating trends like technology and sustainable practices can result in increased revenue and a larger market share.

There is a theory called "MAYA" that is the "Most Advanced Yet Acceptable." The "Father of Industrial Design," Raymond Loewy, is credited with developing this idea. The MAYA principle places emphasis on striking the correct balance between providing people with cutting-edge and inventive content and ensuring that it is both recognizable and acceptable to them. To produce solutions that are both innovative and simple for people to accept, this approach is employed in a variety of fields, including sales theory, communication skills, and product design. In order to ensure that products or ideas are successfully adopted and accepted, the MAYA principle aims to strike a balance between the familiar and the novel by giving users just the right amount of familiarity while introducing new features that are simple to accept

Take the example of the Apple iPhone. By progressively introducing innovations and adjustments with each new generation, Apple's iPhone series demonstrates the MAYA principle while preserving a level of familiarity that users find appealing. Users have been successfully engaged and enthusiastic about the brand's products using this strategy by giving consumers a healthy mix of new features that are simple to use, together with what they already know and understand.

Therefore, a combination of traditional values with innovative trends is essential to meet the changing demands of the market while maintaining core principles for sustained success and growth in the industry.

Unique Niche

A niche refers to a specific area or a specialized market segment where a particular product is sold to a specific group of people. Essentially, a niche can be a unique position that is ideal for an individual or entity.

Broadly, there are three levels of niche: (1) "Macro Level" for e.g., Fashion and Style Business. (2) "Micro Level" for e.g., Men's Clothing. (3) "Nano Level" for e.g., Men's Shirts.

Defining your level of niche gives you the expertise and edge over others and carves the competition out. Targeting a niche market offers several advantages for businesses, like:

Stand Out from the Competition: By focusing on a specific niche market, businesses can differentiate themselves from competitors, making it easier for potential customers to find and engage with them. Niche markets are often underserved, resulting in less competition, which makes it easier for businesses to gain a foothold in the market and stand out from competitors.

Target Specific Group of Customers: Niche marketing allows businesses to better meet the needs and wants of a specific group of customers. This understanding leads to providing better products or services, resulting in more satisfied customers.

Focused Marketing Efforts: Instead of scattering

marketing efforts to reach everyone, targeting a niche market enables businesses to concentrate their marketing strategies effectively, reaching the right audience with tailored messages and allowing for more effective and better products or services, leading to increased profits. A focused approach can maximize profits and ensure long-term success.

Simpler Customer Service: Catering to a niche market allows for more personalized customer service, leading to stronger customer relationships, brand loyalty and repeat business.

To develop a distinctive niche for your product or service, identify and examine your interests and passions. Decide what you are good at or enthusiastic about first. Think about things like your approach to problem-solving, your natural skills, and the subjects you are most interested in studying.

Determine Customer Needs: Recognize the issues and demands of the market you are targeting. To find out about clients' challenges and purchasing habits, conduct market research. Customer personas can be explored with the use of tools that offer insights into how your company might add value.

Study the Competition: Do some research on potential rivals before devoting time and resources to a new venture. This stage assists you in comprehending the state of the market and improving your offering of goods or services.

Establish Your Specialty: Establish a niche that fits with your passions, target market, and competitive landscape after you have a better understanding of these aspects. A targeted group of consumers or businesses interested in a particular product is known as a niche market.

Recognize Who Your Target Audience Is: Become intimately familiar with the thoughts, passions, traits, and particular difficulties that your target market faces. Your product development and marketing efforts will be guided by this information.

Create a Unique Selling Proposition (USP): Construct a USP that sets your company apart from rivals in the industry. Your USP should appeal to your target audience and solve an unmet need in the market.

These will help efficiently to carve out a unique

niche for your product or service, target a certain market, set you apart from competitors, and develop a devoted clientele within that niche market.

> **"Money is only a tool. It will take you wherever you wish, but it will not replace you as the driver."**
>
> **(Ayn Rand)**

Chapter 12

The Wealth Creation - Implementation

Basic Wealth Building Blocks to Start With

IMPLEMENTATION

7. System	8. Leverage		9. Luck
a) Sales Funnel	a) Belief	a) Action	a) Natural
b) Delivery Channels	b) Passion	b) Branding	
	c) Desire	c) Network	

System

If you visit any McDonald's around 7:00 in the evening, you will probably see that it is run by a young adult who is perhaps 19 or 20 years old and has just finished college. Perhaps this 19-year-old's mother doesn't trust him enough to let him drive her car. On the other hand, this same 19-year-old is successfully managing a business that generates more than three million dollars in revenue annually.

Can you tell me the secret? This is what the Air Force uses! Young men and women as young as eighteen are piloting fighter jets that exceed the GDP of several underdeveloped nations. What is the secret?

The secret is called "SYSTEM".

What Alibaba has accomplished in 200 seconds? it sold one billion US dollars. That was remarkable. This was not a covert deal behind the curtains in the midst of night; rather, it involved modest quantities of small commodities pushed into one gigantic and enormous money box in less than 200 seconds. It has demonstrated that "the system" works and the world means business and is ready for it.

A system is characterized as a well-organized group of components or subsystems that work together closely to accomplish a single objective. It starts with a variety of inputs and processes them into outputs that finally achieve the intended outcome.

A business system is a systematic collection of interconnected tasks, procedures, or processes intended to accomplish particular goals in a company. These systems specify the various procedures that are followed in order to reduce workloads, boost output, and guarantee consistency. Standard operating procedures, checklists, and other activities that collaborate to accomplish company objectives are all parts of business systems.

Business systems are necessary to run everyday operations with size and coherence, facilitate the smooth onboarding of new hires, and improve customer service. They support the organization's internal knowledge transfer, guarantee consistency in the delivery of results, and aid in the documentation of crucial processes. In the end, putting in place efficient company systems improves productivity, customer happiness, efficiency, and overall corporate performance.

There are several advantages to putting a business system into place, and they can greatly improve a company's production, efficiency, and overall performance. The following are some main advantages of having and following the system.

Reliable Outcomes: Business processes guarantee that work is done regularly and well, producing consistent results each and every time.

Enhanced Worker Productivity and Performance: Business systems boost worker productivity and performance by simplifying activities and establishing clear standards, which eventually saves time and boosts efficiency.

Save Costs: Documentation of system lowers costly errors, boosts productivity, and eventually lowers operating expenses for the company.

Control and Confidence: Business systems give owners peace of mind that things are going according to plan by giving them the means to keep an eye on and manage important areas of the company without getting too involved.

Growth and Scalability: Robust systems produce valuable assets that can support future growth prospects, franchising, and corporate expansion.

Training and Onboarding: Well-documented systems facilitate the onboarding of new personnel, provide clarity on expectations, and guarantee that staff members are aware of their obligations within the organization.

Continuous Improvement: To increase efficiency

and effectiveness, business processes can be continuously improved and adjusted to new circumstances, technical advancements, and real-world experiences.

Focus and Control: Putting in place efficient business processes aids in keeping a close eye on important company objectives, managing activities, and making sure that resources are distributed as efficiently as possible to produce the intended results.

By putting the system into place, all of the above benefits add up to the business's overall success and expansion.

Leverage

What is leverage?

Those who drive can relate to this! If you have a flat car tyre. What do you do, take out the spare tyre, remove the bolt, lift the car with one hand, place the spare tyre and tighten the bolts? Right... No! Why not? Are you saying that you cannot lift the car with your one hand, not even with two hands? Then what do you do? You place the jack under the car, then use the lever and lift the car up. But how are you able to lift the same car up this time? You are the same person with the same strength, and the car is the same, with the same weight. The answer is a lever. It uses your same power and gets more done. This is called leverage. With minimum effort, you can get it done maximum, to a point which is sometimes not imaginable if you try to do it yourself. The same concept is applied in pullies and cranes to lift tons of weight, which is beyond the human capacity to lift.

Leverage can take many different forms in daily life, allowing people to accomplish more with less time or money. Typical instances of leverage in daily life include the following:

Time Leverage: Making efficient use of other people's time to complete tasks and freeing your personal time for other crucial activities

Skill Leverage: Making the most of each person's unique strengths by utilizing their skills and energy to produce more favorable results.

Personal Life Leverage: Making the most of connections and relationships in one's personal life to achieve objectives and tasks more quickly.

Leverage Technology: The use of technology to boost productivity, automate jobs, and streamline procedures so that people can accomplish more in less time.

System Leverage: Putting procedures and systems in place to streamline operations, cut down on labor, and improve productivity in a variety of spheres of life and work.

In business and wealth creation you can apply various tools to provide you the leverage and get enormous results as well.

Belief Leverage: Belief is a powerful leverage factor, and this concept can be applied to improve behavior, decision-making, and results in a variety of ways in life. Beliefs can be utilized to explore the mind, make wise decisions, and match behaviour with one's own values and objectives.

People who are adept in comprehending and utilizing their beliefs can acquire new perspectives, improve their decision-making, and overcome obstacles in both their personal and professional lives.

By utilizing the motivating factors of pain and pleasure connected to ideas, belief leverage can be a potent instrument for reaching personal objectives. People can successfully match their activities with their values and aims by effectively understanding and exploiting their beliefs.

Following are some aspects where belief leverage can be applied to accomplish personal objectives:

a) **Finding the Points of Pain and Pleasure:** Acknowledge the pleasure and suffering connected to various viewpoints and choices. Leverage the emotional effect of these ideas to propel yourself towards your goals by using this understanding.

b) **Creating Personal Leverage:** Identify areas of discomfort that you may use to your advantage to spur action and reach your objectives. By connecting particular behaviours with intense emotional outcomes, people can motivate themselves to do the required activities to achieve their goals.

c) **Challenging Limiting Beliefs:** Take note

of and confront any limiting beliefs that can prevent you from achieving your objectives. People can get past mental obstacles and get closer to reaching their goals by reframing negative ideas and replacing them with empowering, positive ones.

d) **Beliefs Shaping Experiences:** Recognize how beliefs influence events and results. People can develop a mentality that supports goal achievement and personal development by associating their beliefs with fulfilling experiences and picturing success.

e) **Using Extrinsic and Intrinsic Objectives:** Use motivation and action to propel yourself forward by utilizing your views about extrinsic and intrinsic life objectives. Through the alignment of personal values with objectives that fulfil psychological needs and desires, people can utilize the power of beliefs to drive their own success.

Passion Leverage: The term "passion leverage" describes the strategic application of a person's strong emotional drive or passion to accomplish objectives and propel achievement in a variety of spheres of life, including business. People can go toward their goals with drive and determination if they can harness their passion and make decisions and behaviours that reflect it. The process of directing one's passions' energy and enthusiasm toward worthwhile projects increases attention, dedication, and eventually success in both personal and professional undertakings.

There are several ways in which passion can be used to drive success. Following are some instances of how passion may be applied in the business world as a motivator and a competitive advantage:

a) **Fueling Success:** Passion is a vital component of business success, inspiring people to keep going after their objectives in the face of adversity. It strengthens tenacity and resolve, two traits necessary for long-term business success.

b) **Drawing Others:** Passion is contagious and attract like-minded people to collaborate with you. People are more likely to be inspired and motivated to work with you as partners, investors, or team members when they witness your enthusiasm for what you do.

c) **Increasing Persistence:** People with passion are more likely to persevere through difficulties and disappointments. It acts as a strong force that propels business owners forward in the face of challenges, hard hours, or limited resources.

d) **Motivating Groups:** A passion-driven leader may energize and inspire their group, building a solid and committed team. When team members are inspired and devoted to the company's success, they become more engaged and productive.

e) **Making the Business Unique:** A company can differentiate itself from contemporaries by bringing authenticity, vigour, and direction to its operations through passion. Businesses run by enthusiastic people frequently stand out in the marketplace, drawing clients, financiers, and staff members who share their vision and core principles.

Burning desire leverage: Refers to the strategic use of intense, unwavering passion and determination to propel individuals towards achieving their goals and overcoming obstacles. It involves harnessing a deep, burning desire that serves as a powerful motivator, driving individuals to persist, take bold actions, and remain committed to their objectives even in the face of challenges. By cultivating and leveraging this burning desire, individuals can tap into a high level of energy and focus, ensuring that they stay dedicated and driven towards success in their endeavours.

Leveraging a burning desire in business can yield several benefits that drive success and growth.

a) **Increased Productivity:** A burning desire to succeed can boost motivation and drive individuals to increase their productivity, enabling them to accomplish more in less time

b) **Greater Ambition:** Individuals motivated by a burning desire to reach new heights and inspire others with their vision and ambition.

c) **Improved Resilience:** Working hard towards a passionate goal provides the strength and courage needed to persevere through challenges, enhancing resilience.

d) **Clear Purpose in Life:** A burning desire gives

life structure and purpose, leading to profound satisfaction and contentment when combined with dedication and enthusiasm.

Action Leverage: The skill of "Taking Action" provides leverage in business by enabling individuals to progress towards their goals through consistent and purposeful steps. By actively engaging in tasks and initiatives, individuals can break down complex objectives into manageable parts, leading to incremental progress and eventual success. Taking action empowers individuals to move beyond mere planning and into execution, driving momentum and productivity and results in business endeavours. This proactive approach not only propels individuals towards their goals but also instils a sense of achievement, motivation, and focus that is essential for business growth and success.

Some examples of successful businesses that leveraged the skill of taking action include:

a) **Amazon:** Amazon established itself as a trusted brand and built a vast customer base by taking action early on, making investments in infrastructure and logistics to create an efficient supply chain network. This proactive approach allowed Amazon to gain a competitive edge and dominate various industries beyond retail, such as cloud computing and streaming services.

b) **Uber:** By launching a practical and easy-to-use ride-hailing platform and upending an established market with prompt and decisive action, Uber transformed the transportation sector. Uber quickly became well-known among customers and attained incredible success by quickly growing its network of drivers and constantly innovating.

c) **Tesla:** By being a pioneer in the electric vehicle (EV) market, Tesla leveraged the ability to take action. With its development of high-performance, long-range electric vehicles, Tesla led the way while other automakers were reluctant to make significant investments in EV technologies. With a devoted following and a competitive edge in the market, Tesla was able to position itself as a symbol of sustainability and innovation because of its proactive attitude.

d) **Netflix:** By acting, Netflix upended the long-established video rental industry, which was dominated by Blockbuster, and saw the promise of streaming services early on. With the help of its extensive content library and subscription-based business strategy, Netflix was able to draw in millions of users, make original programming investments, set itself apart from rivals, and take the lead in the streaming market globally.

e) **Google:** Google's success can be attributed to its proactive approach and the skill of taking action. By leveraging its first-mover advantage in the search engine market, Google established itself as a dominant player. Its continuous innovation, strategic decisions, and ability to adapt to changing market dynamics have contributed to its sustained success and market leadership.

These examples illustrate how successful businesses leveraged the skill of taking action to drive innovation, disrupt industries, establish competitive advantages, and achieve remarkable growth and success in their respective markets.

Brand Leverage: The strategic application of an established brand name's power to assist a business's entry into a new but related product category is known as brand leverage. It entails using the power of a brand name to convey important product information to customers. When launching new products, brand leveraging is essential because it gives customers a feeling of familiarity, extends the beneficial aspects of the brand into a new product category, and makes the brand instantly recognizable. By capitalizing on the recognition and reputation of an existing brand, this tactic enables businesses to raise shelf space, lower the cost of launching new items, and improve brand equity.

A business can use a variety of important measures and techniques to assess the effectiveness of a brand-leveraging strategy. The following are some methods for evaluating a brand leveraging strategy's effectiveness:

a) **Awareness of Brands:** To evaluate the effectiveness of a brand leveraging strategy, brand awareness must be tracked. Businesses may gauge the success of their branding initiatives and determine how familiar their target audience is with the brand by monitoring reach and impressions using technologies like web analytics and social media analytics.

b) **Customer Feedback:** Finding out what customers think of a brand's leveraging efforts can be done through focus groups, surveys, and social media interaction. By keeping an eye on customer sentiment, contentment, and engagement, businesses may evaluate how their brand-leveraging strategy is affecting consumer views.

c) **Market Share:** Analyzing market share and contrasting it with rivals can reveal information about how well a brand leveraging strategy is working. Businesses can evaluate how successfully their brand is leveraging efforts by gauging how well it is entering the market and establishing traction in comparison to rivals.

"Self-branding" leverage refers to the strategic use of personal branding to enhance one's reputation, credibility, and visibility in the professional sphere. It involves leveraging one's personal brand attributes, such as skills, expertise, values, and unique qualities, to establish a strong and recognizable personal brand. By effectively utilizing self-branding leverage, individuals can differentiate themselves from others, build a positive reputation, attract opportunities, and create a lasting impact in their chosen field. This strategy enables individuals to showcase their strengths, expertise, and personal brand identity to stand out in a competitive environment and achieve their professional goals.

Businesses can use these metrics and techniques to assess the effectiveness of their brand leveraging strategy, comprehend the effects, sales, revenue, market share, customer feedback, and brand awareness, and make data-driven decisions to maximize the long-term success of their branding initiatives.

Network Leverage describes the thoughtful use of one's professional network to generate opportunities, advance career progress and accomplish organizational goals. It entails making the most of one's network's resources, contacts, and connections in order to gain access to opportunities, support, and important information that can help one succeed personally and make the organization grow. People can broaden their horizons, obtain new perspectives, work together on initiatives, and open doors to new opportunities in their enterprises or occupations by skillfully utilizing their network. This tactic highlights how crucial it is to create and maintain deep relationships in order to get the most out of one's network.

Leveraging the network can help in:

a) **Access to Resources:** Leveraging your network allows you to gain access to valuable resources, such as funding, expertise, and support, that can help you achieve your goals and advance your career.

b) **Building Credibility and Trust:** By utilizing your network, you can build credibility and trust with potential investors, partners, and clients. Personal connections that vouch for you can enhance your reputation and make it easier for others to trust in your vision and abilities.

c) **Saving Time:** Leveraging existing connections can save you time in various processes, such as fundraising or finding the right people for your venture. Instead of searching for potential investors or attending numerous networking events, leveraging your network helps you quickly identify suitable opportunities and connections.

d) **Staying Informed:** Networking allows you to stay connected and informed about industry trends, market insights, and valuable feedback that can help you make informed decisions and stay ahead in your field.

e) **Personal Growth:** Networking provides opportunities to seek alternative perspectives, new ideas, and challenges that can enhance both personal and professional development. Engaging with diverse individuals in your network can broaden your knowledge base and improve problem-solving skills.

f) **Enhanced Visibility:** Regularly meeting with people in your network or attending industry events can help build your personal brand and increase visibility within your industry or market. A broader network can lead to more people who know you and can vouch for you when needed.

Natural Luck

As we have discussed in the chapter "The Luck Design", there are people who do not have wealth acumen built in them naturally, but they are not willing to submit to the pain of poverty and lack and are aware of their ability to learn and change their adverse circumstances. They are lucky enough to have this awareness that they can turn the tables. This is what is called natural luck. You take action, do hard work, and use your abilities, and luck will start activating in your life by attracting opportunities and desirable results.

Remember, we cannot fight with the guys enjoying Divine and Inherent Luck, and guys suffering from unfortunate luck are not willing to do anything and change themselves as they are not aware of their own worth and potential. That leaves us with those who are not willing to settle with their current adverse circumstances and are eager to find out the way towards wealth and abundance. These are the real and natural lucky ones.

One of the greatest discoveries a man has made, one of his great surprises, is to find he can do what he was afraid he couldn't do.

(Henry Ford)

Chapter 13

The Future History

THE FUTURE HISTORY

Thirty years from now, from the deck of your Space Ship Galactica, while travelling to your new home on planet Fortunica Dignica, reading from the book authored by you, a page from the history when you refused to surrender 30 years back to the life of bondage and decided to take control of your life back to make a difference in the world. You are converting into history at a fast pace, and the pen to write your future history is in your hands right now.

There are millions of people out there in the world who are just waiting to complete their days in this world till they lie on their death bed when they suddenly become wise enough to realize that they could have written the story of respect and prosperity on their page of history and avoided the life of insult, pain and suffering when they had a choice. But they have no tomorrows left with them now. They are not realizing now that they are heading towards the biggest problem in the world, that "Time" is running out.

The Game of Clicker!

The game of clicker will continue if they do not challenge it. What is the game of clicker?

The most dangerous thing that affects any living being is the state of lack and prolonged hunger, which destroys the thinking ability and sanity of a person and makes the mind numb. There is a technique that animal trainers use to tame animals to dance to their tune; they keep them hungry for a certain length of time, then click the clicker and give them a feed. This is called the clicker technique, based on behavioural psychology, on getting desirable behaviour and rewarding it. Continuous hunger and lack of food after a certain period is unbearable to the extent that the subject is prepared to do anything from losing self-respect to accepting slavery.

The difference between animal and humans is that human beings have superior mental faculties and if they decide, they can break this deadly and horrible trap by using their intellect and wisdom as thinking stimulates the mind and encourage people to question their condition and change them accordingly.

There are two biggest incidents that happens in everyone's life. One has already happened (Your Birth), and the second is about to happen.

In order to take control of your life and respect, work so hard, so hard, so hard that Divine stop doing everything, turn around and look at you and ask, who is this person?

Within, you have the capability to learn anything and have inborn talents and potential to change your life. What is the difference between the value of 1 kg of gold and 1 penny lying in the depths of an ocean bed? There is no difference; they do not have any value and have the same worth; they are just equal. It is when they come out of the ocean that their value is established, and people come to know that gold is gold and a penny is just a penny. As long as your talents remain inside you, they have no value and worth. You have to take them out and apply to get a high bid on them.

Trim Tabs

Yes, it is true that you cannot suddenly make big changes in your life immediately, but you can start with small improvements and make small changes in your life, which can lead to big results and outcomes. If you have seen the oil tankers in the ocean, these are huge ships approximately 450 meters long and carry around 250,000 tons of crude oil. In order to change the direction of the ship, the navigator has to move the main rudder, which is around 100 tons in weight, and there is no way a human being can move it against the water current flowing underneath. Along with the main rudder there are small rudders of 100 pounds in weight called "trim tabs", which can easily be moved by the navigator. These small trim tabs change the direction of the strong water current towards the main rudder and help it to turn around and change the direction of the oil tankers. You need to work like trim tabs to make small shifts in your life to have a big turnaround in the direction of your life.

Chestnut Smile

In the late 18th century, a reign of terror was established following the French Revolution; forty thousand people were sentenced to guillotine. It became a public attraction to see heads chopped off every day. One day, the chief justice of the revolution council was going to his chamber when he saw a small girl sitting on the stairs of the court building selling chestnuts. As the chief justice saw the girl, the girl smiled at him. This melted the heart of the justice and he stopped issuing the death warrants. Your small efforts, your little smiles, and your genshai acts can bring a huge change in the world. Remember, all flights take off from Earth only; all greatness rises from humbleness. Understand your value and worth.

Plan to Change Your Life.

Don't just sit crossing the fingers, don't suffer and stay agonize in life. Make a plan and strategy to change your life.

If you do not make a plan to change your life, **you will become a part of someone else's plan forever.** And trust me, other's plans for you are not so compassionate and appreciative of you. Dare to be great and make a plan about yourself. As Jim Rohn says, "Let others lead small lives, but not you. Let others argue over small things, but not you. Let others cry over small hurts, but not you. Let others leave their future in someone else's hands but not you."

Next ten years will definitely pass in your life and you will surely reach another ten years of life, question is where? If you do not have plan if you don't know where you are heading? Are you reading the books? are you learning any skills, are you making yourself visible and viable to create some value in the life of others?

As they say your life is the average of five people you spend most of your time with in every respect, the skills you have, the wealth you have, the respect you have and the health you have. Have you decided to change your circle of influence to be associated with the winners and champs'? Have you decided to adopt the habits of successful and highly effective people in your life?

Money and Painful Reality

In the search of subsistence or sustenance, a place to place, door to door, city to city, country to country, man jostles and suffer. This chase has stolen from his lips the blooming honey smile, the refreshing and joyous talking style, the fragrance of words, the radiant beauty and glow of eyes and the singing soul away.

When his world is dark and colourless, he wonders why the world smiles? he wonders why when people meet, party and socialize and are happy. He wonders why, when he himself dislikes the gatherings.

Once a blossom soul is now a fading flower with a pale face, the sweet words turn into agony and anger, the cultured voice is changed to abusive; the singing soul is now a song of death.

There are many factors among others which increases or tarnish the self-esteem, but money is most influential and dominant among them, due to its strong purchasing power. The money has taken away from us a human and humanity as well.

Please remember, you are not so cheap to be reduced to rubble in one and the only life you have. The "Idea Human" is the greatest project of the universe. Human talents have always amazed humans, and recognizing them is one of them.

Whatever your concept of success is, everyone wants to be successful. No one want to be a failure, from religious perspective salvation is success, for some richness is success, for other reaching the summit of world highest peak is the success, for some Olympic gold is success, while others attribute success to having children, losing weight and having goods. No one surely likes failure.

We have seen and discussed throughout the book the formulas and universal laws of success to achieve anything, which are applied in the lives of successful people. If you apply the same laws and put in your best efforts and still do not succeed, then it is not your failure; it is the failure of the laws and the failure of the Divine Supreme, who is the designer and architect of the laws of success.

Think about that, as much as you like to be successful and don't like failure for yourself, do you think that

Divine Supreme likes failure for himself, by making false and dishonest laws of success?

> **"Our greatest weakness lies in giving up.**
> **The most certain way to succeed**
> **is always to try just one more time."**
>
> **(Thomas Edison)**

Conclusion

Life is the game of understanding the two beings, self-being and divine being.

There is no such thing as something for nothing. Everything of value comes at a price. The world is already overflowing with too many broke intellectuals (people who know how to play the game but refuse to get out on the field and actually PLAY). So don't become a professional student.

Knowing Without Acting Is Like Not Knowing At All!!!

So, the price you will have to pay for the value you seek from this book is mastering the information contained in it. And true mastery cannot take place only intellectually, it must be actually **experienced.**

So, the challenge to you is to take this very valuable information and put it into action. Don't blow it off as something that won't work just because it didn't cost you a fortune or you didn't have to go to school for 4 years to learn it. It's probably the single most valuable or profitable tool you will ever own...IF ... you use it!

By using this information and creating new habits this will become second nature to you. You've got to dedicate yourself to mastering what is revealed to you here.

So. Practice ...Practice... Practice – until it becomes automatic!

I'll leave you now with this question?

When you leave planet Earth, what would you like your legacy to be for future generations?

> **Be like a postage stamp.**
> **Stick to one thing until you get there.**
>
> **(Josh Billings)**

If you benefit from this book and wish to give your testimonial, recommendation, comments or suggestions, you can write to badararshi@gmail.com with your name, designation and phone number. Your testimonial can be published in later editions.

www.ingramcontent.com/pod-product-compliance
Lightning Source LLC
Chambersburg PA
CBHW021427150726
47989CB00001B/143